CHAMPIONS

CHAMPIONS

Stories of Ten Remarkable Athletes

by Bill Littlefield

Paintings by Bernie Fuchs

With a Foreword by Frank Deford

Little, Brown and Company
Boston   New York   London

To Amy and Alison, who'll like the stories,
I hope, and to Mary, who's listened patiently
to so many of them

Text copyright © 1993 by Bill Littlefield
Illustrations copyright © 1993 by Bernie Fuchs

First Edition

"To Satch," by Samuel W. Allen, is used by permission of the author.

Library of Congress Cataloging-in-Publication Data

Littlefield, Bill.
    Champions : stories of ten remarkable athletes / by Bill Littlefield ;
  paintings by Bernie Fuchs ; with a foreword by Frank Deford.
        p.   cm.
    Includes index.
    Summary: A collection of sports profiles exploring athletes who
  have made extraordinary achievements, grown beyond their successes,
  and given something back to their sports.
        ISBN 0-316-52805-6 (cl)
        ISBN 0-316-55849-4 (pb)
    2. Athletes — Biography — Juvenile literature. [1. Athletes.]
    I. Fuchs, Bernie, ill.   II. Title.
    GV697.A1L58   1993
    796'.092'2 — dc20
    [B]   92-31390

  10 9 8 7 6 5 4 3 2
  NIL

  Printed in Italy

796.092
L

Contents

Acknowledgments vi

Foreword by Frank Deford vii

Introduction ix

Satchel Paige · *Baseball Pitcher* 1

Julie Krone · *Jockey* 11

Edson Arantes do Nascimento ("Pelé") · *Soccer Player* 25

Joan Benoit Samuelson · *Runner* 39

Nate "Tiny" Archibald · *Basketball Player* 53

Susan Butcher · *Dogsled Racer* 67

Muhammad Ali · *Boxer* 81

Billie Jean King · *Tennis Player* 93

Diana Golden · *Skier* 105

Roberto Clemente · *Baseball Player* 117

Suggested Reading 130

Index 132

Acknowledgments

The articles and books listed at the end of this book have been enormously useful, particularly the excellent biography of Muhammad Ali, the fine *Sports Illustrated* pieces on Julie Krone and Diana Golden, and the *Boston Globe Magazine* article on Susan Butcher. My thanks to Thomas Hauser, Gary Smith, Meg Lukens, Susan Trausch, and all the other writers who've told stories of these ten athletes.

Many people have helped in one way or another or offered advice as I was writing this book, among them Gail Shank, Kathy Russell, Elaine Bernier, Cathy King, and the rest of the librarians at Curry College; Richard Lapchick and Joanne Legg from the Center for the Study of Society and Sport at Northeastern University; Dick Johnson and Saul Wisnia at the New England Sports Museum; Sally Baker; Amby Burfoot; the Boston Athletic Association; the National Basketball Hall of Fame; Dave Cowens; Marlene Samuelson; Raymond and Peter Hainer; Leah Levin Beeferman; Paula Cabral; Gabe Rice; Steve Murray; and Dave Summergrad and his students.

Thanks, also, to Mark Schramm, my excellent editor at National Public Radio, for reading and commenting on the material.

I'm grateful to the Curry College Chapter of the American Association of University Professors and the college administration for negotiating a process for granting release time to teachers with projects to pursue, and to Dean David Fedo for agreeing that this particular project was a worthy one.

Thanks, finally, to Ann Rider, who came up with the original idea that I bent into this book.

Foreword

It never troubles me in the slightest that children or teenagers make heroes of their favorite athletes. Now, yes, I certainly would be suspicious of an adult who put a shortstop or linebacker on a pedestal, but then, I would also be just as put off by any kid who worshiped a politician or a preacher. There's plenty of time for that sort of ponderous solemnity when we get older and watch the late news.

There are, in fact, many natural reasons why real children should properly fall for athletes. For example: sports stars look great. They're on television. They're out of high school and they don't have pimples, but they're not officially grown-up yet. Athletes are benign warriors. They must perform with the whole world watching — and there is a basic nobility to that. And also, of course, as everybody knows, they make a lot of money and wear cool clothes.

From another point of view, be realistic. If not sports stars, then whom else would normal children look up to? The choices are: (1) rock stars, (2) TV sitcom characters, especially the ones on the Fox network, and (3) cartoon people.

Yet I also do believe that children are not conned. They understand that even champions are, as human beings, not quite formed yet. Children may make heroes of their sports stars, but likewise they appreciate their fragility. When I was a boy, I idolized some young men who wore numbers on their backs, but I also learned early on that even the best baseball players make outs two-thirds of the time. I also had a pretty good idea that while my heroes worked at baseball or football, they also liked girls and stuff. When heroes behave somewhat erratically in their private life, I don't think children are let down nearly as much as moralists who use that dreadful term *role model* woefully declare they are.

The heroes in Bill Littlefield's book all triumph over obstacles, and many of them triumph over failures as well. But I think it's more important for a child to grasp the notion so evident in these pages that even the greatest champions continue to triumph *in tandem* with failure. Champions may be larger than life, but they are never above life. And that is what these stories illustrate so well.

They also instruct us in an even simpler reality: that people who become famous and successful all come from somewhere . . . usually, in fact, from somewhere pretty mundane. Just like you and me. Children are pretty good at understanding that people grow up, but they're not so good at understanding how people also can move up. Littlefield's stories all possess a sort of warm neo–Horatio Alger quality that helps any young reader see better that, yes, you can get there from here.

Frank Deford

Introduction

It's a little silly to refer to athletes as heroes, but it's easy to understand why it happens. They do things the rest of us can't do. They hit fastballs coming at them at ninety-five miles an hour. They leap into the air and seem to defy gravity, then they swoop like monstrous birds toward the basket, slam the ball through the hoop, and somehow return to earth unharmed. For their efforts they are paid millions of dollars, which is certainly hero-size money. Their faces are reproduced everywhere, and their words are repeated and preserved. Likenesses of some of them are cast in bronze or chipped out of stone and displayed in halls of fame.

Our best athletes fire our imaginations. Within their games they give us images of excellence, which are often hard to find elsewhere. But the most admirable of our athletes do even more. They demonstrate in their work such qualities as perseverance and grace under pressure. And these qualities don't desert them when they leave the playing field. The stories of their lives give us patterns, and from these patterns we can learn something about finding a passion and working hard and believing in ourselves. And as the accomplished athletes move past the days of their triumphs, they must find ways to make meaningful lives while the crowds cheer for somebody else. That's part of the pattern, too: moving beyond the glory.

Each of the athletes whose stories make up this book is an individual, of course, but the tales share some circumstances and qualities. Roberto Clemente's father made his son's first baseball bat by hand, and Billie Jean King's father carved a bat for her, too, during the years before she switched to tennis. Edson Arantes do Nascimento ("Pelé") and Nate "Tiny" Archibald both came from poverty so unrelenting that it crushed many of the children with whom they grew up. Satchel Paige and Muhammad Ali both endured racial slurs and violent threats from white people who hated them for being black, successful, and proud. Julie Krone and Susan Butcher each had to hammer away at barriers created by men who didn't believe women had any place in their sports.

But there are remarkable contrasts within this group, too. Pelé's formal education ended in the fourth grade, and Julie Krone's conviction that she was ready to be a jockey at fifteen led her to quit school. On the other hand, Joan Benoit Samuelson treasures her college days at Bowdoin, and Tiny Archibald has worked to earn his Ph.D. and become *Dr.* Tiny Archibald. Pelé and Archibald drew some of their strength from the challenge of escaping poverty, but Diana Golden grew up in an exclusive Boston suburb, and it didn't hurt her courage and strength a bit.

Some of the athletes considered in this book talk thoughtfully and compellingly about how they have become who they are. Diana Golden's cheerful and steadfast insistence that she is neither heroic nor even particularly courageous represents an attitude from which all athletes and all fans who glorify them can learn. Joan Benoit Samuelson's graceful adjustment to celebrity has been similarly admirable. Not many other athletes — or insurance salespeople or short-order cooks, for that matter — would say, "Winning is neither everything nor the only thing; it is one of many things." It's a piece of wisdom that hints at Joan Benoit Samuelson's remarkable determination to keep her athletic achievements in perspective. She understands herself as a thoughtful and sensitive citizen of the planet who happens to be able to train herself to run long distances faster than almost anyone else, happens to love doing it, and therefore feels blessed.

Sports provide individuals with the opportunity to challenge themselves and each other, and sometimes even to challenge those of us who are watching. Jackie Robinson, Satchel Paige, Larry Doby, and the rest of the first generation of black major leaguers challenged people who believed that the races should not be mixed on the ball field or in the locker room, or on the bus or in the restaurant where the team ate, or at the hotel where the players slept. Billie Jean King pushed and pulled women's tennis toward parity with the men's game and changed the way we understand not only women's tennis and women's sports but women themselves. Tiny Archibald has challenged the prejudices of folks who would dismiss pro athletes as self-centered, shortsighted, and disinclined to pay much attention to their own education or the needs of those less fortunate than themselves. And Diana Golden has sent us to the dictionary in search of a term to replace *disabled.*

Each of these champions has found in sports a way to fuse joy, hard work, and the relentless determination to excel and excel again. They have managed for long moments to erase the distinction between work and play. What a remarkable thing! For most of us they cannot literally be role models, because we do not have the physical gifts to do what they have done. But in a larger sense they do perhaps provide us with a sense of how to build lives that are made up of passion, dedication, self-respect, and constant striving. And of course, early in each of these lives is a child's dream. Perhaps one other thing that these stories can teach us is that imagination is essential, and that every champion was once a dreaming child.

Satchel Paige

Leroy "Satchel" Paige, perhaps the greatest pitcher ever, came out of the Negro leagues, where there'd been a Babe Ruth named Josh Gibson and a Rickey Henderson named James "Cool Papa" Bell. By the time the major leagues finally allowed him to play, in 1948, Paige should have been too old, too slow, and too beat up to get anybody out. But for a few remarkable and flamboyant seasons with Cleveland and St. Louis, he showed folks what they'd been missing during all those years of segregated baseball. Maybe Satchel was lucky to finally have his chance, but the fans who saw him take advantage of it were luckier, and none of them ever forgot it.

I threw my trouble ball, and they just wet their pants or cried. They thought of passing a law against me.

— *Satchel Paige*

LATE IN THE AFTERNOON of July 9, 1948, Leroy "Satchel" Paige began the long walk from the bullpen to the mound at Cleveland's Municipal Stadium. He didn't hurry. He *never* hurried. As he said himself, he "kept the juices flowing by jangling gently" as he moved. The crowd roared its appreciation. This was the fellow they'd come to see.

When Satchel finally reached the mound, Cleveland manager Lou Boudreau took the ball from starting pitcher Bob Lemon, who would eventually be voted into the Hall of Fame but had tired that day, and gave it to Paige. Probably he said something like, "Shut 'em down, Satchel." Whatever he said, Paige had no doubt heard the words a thousand times. Though he was a rookie with the Indians that year, no pitcher in the history of baseball had ever been more thoroughly prepared for a job. He kicked at the rubber, looked in for the sign, and got set to throw. In a moment, twenty-odd years later than it should have happened, Satchel Paige would deliver his first pitch in the big leagues.

The tall, skinny kid named Leroy Paige became Satchel Paige one day at the railroad station in Mobile, Alabama. He was carrying bags for the folks getting on and off the trains, earning all the nickels and dimes he could to help feed his ten brothers and sisters. Eventually it occurred to him that if he slung a pole across his narrow shoulders and hung the bags, or satchels, on the ends of the pole, he could carry for more people at once and collect more nickels and dimes. It worked, but it looked a little funny. "You look like some kind of ol' satchel tree," one of his friends told him, and the nickname stuck.

Even in those days, before he was a teenager, Satchel Paige could throw hard and accurately. Years later, Paige swore that when his mother would send him out into the yard to get a chicken for dinner, he would brain the bird with a rock. "I used to kill *flying* birds with rocks, too," he said. "Most people need shotguns to do what I did with rocks."

It was not a talent that would go unnoticed for long. He was pitching for the semipro Mobile Tigers before he was eighteen . . . or maybe before he was sixteen, or before he was twelve. There is some confusion about exactly when Satchel Paige was born, and Satchel never did much to clarify the matter. But there never has been any confusion about whether he could pitch. His first steady job in baseball was with the Chattanooga Black Lookouts. He was paid fifty dollars a month. In the seasons that followed he would also pitch for the Birmingham Black Barons, the Nashville Elite Giants, the Baltimore Black Sox, the Pittsburgh Crawfords, and the Kansas City Monarchs, among other teams.

If those names are not as familiar sounding as those of the New York Yankees, the Los Angeles Dodgers, or the Boston Red Sox, it's because they were all clubs in the Negro leagues, not the major leagues. Today the presence of black baseball players in the big leagues is taken for granted. Hank Aaron is the greatest of the home run hitters, and Rickey Henderson has stolen more bases than any other big leaguer. But before 1947, neither of them would have had the opportunity to do what they have done. Until Brooklyn Dodger general manager Branch Rickey signed Jackie Robinson, black players had no choice but to play for one of the all-black teams, and making that choice, they faced hardships no major-leaguer today could imagine.

Players in the Negro leagues crowded into broken-down cars and bumped over rutted roads to makeshift ball fields with lights so bad

that every pitch was a potential weapon. Then they drove all night for an afternoon game three hundred miles away. On good days they played before big, appreciative crowds in parks they'd rented from the major league teams in Chicago, New York, or Pittsburgh. On bad days they learned that the team they were playing for was too broke to finish the season, and they would have to look for a healthier team that could use them, or else find a factory job.

It took talent, hard work, and a sense of humor to survive in the Negro leagues, and Satchel Paige had a lot of all three. But he didn't just survive. He prospered. Everybody knows about the fastball, the curve, and the slider. But Satchel threw a "bee" ball, which, he said, "would always *be* where I wanted it to *be*." He featured a trouble ball, which, of course, gave the hitters a lot of trouble. Even the few who could see it couldn't hit it. Sometimes he'd come at them with his hesitation pitch, a delivery so mysterious that the man at the plate would sometimes swing before the ball left Satchel's hand.

Nor was pitching his sole triumph. Early in his career Satchel Paige began building a reputation as a storyteller, a spinner of tall tales as well as shutouts. He particularly liked to recall an occasion upon which he was asked to come on in relief of a pitcher who'd left men on first and third with nobody out. "It was a tight situation," Satchel would say.

We only had a one-run lead, and that was looking mighty slim. But I had an idea. When I left the bench, I stuck a baseball in my pocket, so when the manager gave me the game ball on the mound, I had two. I went into my stretch just like usual. Then I threw one ball to first and the other to third. It was a good pickoff move, you see, and it fooled the batter, too. He swung, even though there was no ball to swing at. Those boys at first and third were both out, of course, and the umpire called strike three on the batter, so that was it for the inning. It's always good to save your strength when you can.

Major-leaguers today make enough money so that they don't have to work over the winter, but it hasn't always been so. Big-leaguers and Negro-leaguers alike used to make extra money after their regular seasons ended by putting together makeshift teams and playing each other wherever they could draw a paying crowd. This practice was called barnstorming, and Satchel Paige was the world champion at it. For thirty years, from 1929 to 1958, he played baseball summer and winter. When it was too cold to play in the Negro league cities, he played in Cuba, Mexico, and the Dominican Republic. In Venezuela he battled a boa constrictor in the outfield, or so he said, and in Ciudad Trujillo he dodged the machine-gun fire of fans who'd bet on the losing team.

Throughout the early years of these adventures, the years of Satchel's prime, he often barnstormed against the best white ballplayers of his day. St. Louis Cardinal great Dizzy Dean once told him, "You're a better pitcher than I ever hope to be." Paige beat Bob Feller and struck out Babe Ruth. And when Joe DiMaggio, considered by some the most multitalented ballplayer ever, beat out an infield hit against Paige in 1936, DiMaggio turned to his teammates and said, "Now I know I can make it with the Yankees. I finally got a hit off of ol' Satch."

Everywhere these confrontations took place, Satchel Paige would hear the same thing: "If only you were white, you'd be a star in the big leagues." The fault, of course, was not with Satchel. The fault and the shame were with major league baseball, which stubbornly, stupidly clung to the same prejudice that characterized many institutions in the United States besides baseball. Prejudice has not yet disappeared from the game. Black players are far less likely than their white counterparts to be hired as managers or general managers. But today's black players can thank Robinson, Paige, and a handful of other pioneers for the opportunities they enjoy.

Though the color line prevented Satchel Paige from pitching in the company his talent and hard work should have earned for him, he was not bitter or defeated. Ignorant white fans would sometimes taunt him, but he kept their insults in perspective. "Some of them would call you 'nigger,' " he said of his early years on the road, "but most of them would cheer you." Years later he worked to shrug off the pain caused by the restaurants that would not serve him, the hotels that would not rent him a room, the fans who would roar for his bee ball but would not acknowledge him on the street the next day. "Fans all holler the same at a ball game," he would say, as if the racists and the racist system had never touched him at all.

When he finally got the chance to become the first black pitcher in the American League at age forty-two (or forty-six, or forty-eight), he made the most of it. On that first day in Cleveland, Satchel Paige did the job he'd never doubted he could do. First he smiled for all the photographers. Then he told the butterflies in his stomach to leave off their flapping around. Then he shut down the St. Louis Browns for two innings before being lifted for a pinch hitter.

And still there were doubters. "Sure," they said to each other the next day when they read the sports section. "The old man could work two innings against the Browns. Who couldn't?"

But Satchel Paige fooled 'em, as he'd been fooling hitters for twenty-five years and more. He won a game in relief six days later, his first major league win. Then on August 3 he started a game against the Washington Senators before 72,000 people. Paige went seven innings and won. In his next two starts he threw shutouts against the Chicago White Sox, and through the waning months of that summer, his only complaint was that he was "a little tired from underwork."

The routine on the major league level must have been pretty leisurely for a fellow who'd previously pitched four or five times a week.

Satchel Paige finished the 1948 season with six wins and only one loss. He'd allowed the opposing teams an average of just over two runs a game. Paige was named Rookie of the Year, an honor he might well have achieved twenty years earlier if he'd had the chance. The sportswriters of the day agreed that without Satchel's contribution, the Indians, who won the pennant, would have finished second at best. Many of the writers were dismayed when Satchel appeared for only two-thirds of an inning in the World Series that fall. Paige, too, was disappointed that the manager hadn't chosen to use him more, but he was calm in the face of what others might have considered an insult. The writers told him, "You sure take things good." Satchel smiled and said, "Ain't no other way to take them."

Satchel Paige outlasted the rule that said he couldn't play in the big leagues because he was black. Then he made fools of the people who said he couldn't get major league hitters out because he was too old. But his big league numbers over several years — twenty-eight wins and thirty-two saves — don't begin to tell the story of Paige's unparalleled career. Playing for teams that no longer exist in leagues that came and went with the seasons, Satchel Paige pitched in some 2,500 baseball games. Nobody has ever pitched in more. And he had such fun at it. Sometimes he'd accept offers to pitch in two cities on the same day. He'd strike out the side for three innings in one game, then fold his long legs into his car and race down the road toward the next ballpark. If the police could catch him, they would stop him for speeding. But when they recognized him, as often as not they'd escort him to the second game with sirens howling, well aware that there might be a riot in the park if Satchel Paige didn't show up as advertised. Once he'd arrived, he'd instruct his infielders and outfielders to sit down for an inning, then he'd strike out the side again.

For his talent, his energy, and his showmanship, Satchel Paige was the most famous of the Negro league players, but when he got some measure of recognition in the majors, he urged the writers to remember that there had been lots of other great ballplayers in those Negro league games. He named them, and he told their stories. He made their exploits alive and real for generations of fans who'd never have known.

In 1971, the Baseball Hall of Fame in Cooperstown, New York, inducted Satchel Paige. The action was part of the Hall's attempt to remedy baseball's shame, the color line. The idea was to honor Paige and some of the other great Negro league players like Josh Gibson and Cool Papa Bell, however late that honor might come. Satchel Paige could have rejected that gesture. He could have told the baseball establishment that what it was doing was too little, too late. But when the time came for Satchel Paige to speak to the crowd gathered in front of the Hall of Fame to celebrate his triumphs, he told the people, "I am the proudest man on the face of the earth today."

Satchel Paige, whose autobiography was entitled *Maybe I'll Pitch Forever,* died in Kansas City in 1982. He left behind a legend as large as that of anyone who ever played the game, as well as a long list of achievements celebrated in story and song — and in at least one fine poem, by Samuel Allen:

To Satch

Sometimes I feel like I will *never* stop
Just go on forever
Till one fine mornin'
I'm gonna reach up and grab me a handfulla stars
Swing out my long lean leg
And whip three hot strikes burnin' down the heavens
And look over at God and say
How about that!

Julie Krone

When Julie Krone would tell her junior high school classmates that she was going to be a jockey, they'd laugh at her. Then one of them would have to hold her off at arm's length while she threw helpless windmill punches. On the first day she went to the track to hustle up a ride, the men at the gate turned her away. They figured she was too young even to watch the ponies legally, and they laughed when she protested. But since those days, Julie Krone has made more than two thousand trips to the winner's circle.

Am I afraid? It's a good question. If someone could find out, I guess none of us would be riding. All of us are aware of the danger all the time. You hope you'll be the lucky one.

— *Julie Krone*

J UDI KRONE, mother of two-year-old Julianne Louise Krone, had a horse to sell. She didn't much like the idea. She preferred training her horses, or exercising them, even feeding them, to selling them. But she needed the eight hundred dollars the palomino might bring, and she had a customer.

"I want to teach my children to ride," the customer said. "I need a gentle horse. Are you sure this horse is gentle?"

"I'm here to tell you this is a sweet horse," said Judi Krone.

"She's a little bigger than I'd like," the customer said.

"But look at those sleepy ol' eyes," Judi Krone said. "Look at how quiet she stands."

"I don't know . . ." the customer mumbled.

Darn it, Krone thought, I'm gonna lose her. And then she looked down at her daughter, Julie, barefoot and diapered beside her, and had an idea. She picked Julie up and plopped her on the palomino's back. The horse didn't mind, and though she'd never been in the saddle before, Julie seemed to take to it.

"There, you see?" said Judi Krone to her customer.

The palomino must have thought she'd said, "Giddyup." She took a lazy look over her shoulder to see who was aboard, seemed to shrug as if to say, "If it's okay with you, it's okay with me," and started off across the riding ring at a gentle trot. Bouncing gently in the saddle, Julie giggled happily. When the palomino reached the other side of the ring, she stopped, as if awaiting instructions. The tiny girl on her back reached for the reins and pulled them. The horse turned obediently and stepped back toward the little girl's mother and the customer, who was reaching for her checkbook.

Looking back, it must have seemed to Judi as if her daughter had hardly stopped riding after that day. Julie found joy in it that she found nowhere else. The children she knew as she got older made fun of her size — she was always tiny for her age — and her voice, which was high and squeaky. But her mother's horses never made fun of her, and when she rode them she was tall and strong. She polished their hooves and combed their manes and rode in shows. She rode them bareback and barefoot in the morning before breakfast. She ran home from school to ride them before changing her clothes. When it was time to come in for dinner, she'd point the one she was riding toward the barn, stand up in the stirrups, and gallop, standing, toward the big door, falling into the saddle only a half second before she would have decapitated herself. In junior high school she rode well enough to earn a job with a circus as a trick rider, but at the last moment she decided maybe she wouldn't run away from home that week after all.

Still, it's an almost unimaginably long way from bobbing around the riding ring on an eight-hundred-dollar nag to guiding some millionaire's precious investment of a Thoroughbred down the homestretch while a dozen other horses and jockeys try to beat you to the finish line. The easy wisdom at the racetrack had always been that women didn't belong on horseback, except perhaps as exercise girls. Sure, some of them were good with horses, gentle with them and kind. But what good would those qualities do a woman who got caught between two of the twelve-hundred-pound beasts going into a tight turn? What happened when these women riders needed the strength to hold back a mount that was leaning into another horse, endangering horses and riders all around? And what about the nerve it took to shoot through the tiny gap between horses that might open up for just a second or two, then close into a vise if you weren't clear on the other side? Where was a woman going to find the courage to enter that gap and the muscle to kick the horse through it?

Questions like these dogged the women who preceded Julie Krone at the Thoroughbred tracks, and sometimes the questions were the least of their worries. In 1968, Kathy Kusner had to take the Maryland racing establishment to court before she could get a license to ride. The same year, Penny Ann Early faced a boycott at Churchill Downs, where the Kentucky Derby is run, though lots of less talented men got mounts. Then there was Barbara Jo Rubin at Tropical Park in Miami. In 1969 the cowards who didn't want her to ride threw rocks at the trailer she lived in, hoping to scare her off. Robyn Smith and a few other female jockeys succeeded for a while elsewhere, most notably at the New York tracks, but the combination of mean circumstances and lack of opportunity discouraged most of them pretty quickly.

Maybe the stories of those discouragements were the only horse stories Julie Krone's mother didn't read her. Because discouragement didn't seem to be part of the program for Julie, at least not as far as her dream of racing horses was concerned. She was, as time passed, increasingly discouraged by lots of other things. She was a teenager without a boyfriend, partly because the boys in her class were embarrassed to ask out a girl who still bought her clothes in the children's section of the store and who looked like a hopeless impostor whenever she put on makeup. The real world of Cokes after school and who was going to the dance with whom had no place for her. So she made up her own world of stunts on horseback and stories in which she rode champions — great-hearted horses who didn't care that she was small and sounded funny. When her parents were divorced and her brother left home to live with their father, Julie spent more time with the horses than ever before, and she got better at riding them every day.

And her mother didn't much worry. The woman who'd put her two-year-old on the palomino's back just crossed her fingers and hoped that Julie's one passion, which was also her escape and her reason for getting out of bed each morning, would lead somewhere. No wonder, then, that when Julie announced at fifteen that she wanted to leave home and try to get a job caring for and exercising horses at Churchill Downs, her mother nodded okay and more. Students were supposed to be sixteen before they could leave school to work, but Julie's mother altered her fifteen-year-old daughter's birth certificate, and nobody in Kentucky ever noticed.

Her first professional riding experience came the following year, after she'd moved on to Tampa Bay Downs in Florida. On the day she arrived there, the guards at the gate wouldn't let her in, figuring she was too young even to *watch* horses run, but she climbed over the fence. Once inside, Julie wandered around until a woman who was a friend of one of the horse trainers saw her and assumed she was a lost child. In a way, the woman was right, but Julie wasn't buying that. "I'm gonna be a jockey," she told the trainer, whose name was Jerry Pace.

"If you say so," Pace said. For the heck of it, he let her ride one of his horses around the training track. But he recognized a natural when he saw one. All the hours of stunts and races against imaginary opponents and ducking under the barn door with no time to spare had not been in vain. Jerry Pace got the little girl who couldn't get past the guards a couple of rides, and five weeks later, Julie Krone was in the winner's circle on a forgettable horse named Lord Farckle. As the tired, bored track photographer snapped the traditional picture of the winning horse and jockey, Julie Krone worked hard to look as if it was no big deal — nothing but winning a two-bit race on a slow day at a second-rate track. But she sure liked the feeling of kicking home a winner, and she couldn't wait to get to work at bringing one around again. Almost before she'd dismounted Lord Farckle, she be-

gan begging and scrounging for more rides. She got forty-seven more of them before the meeting at Tampa Bay Downs closed. She brought in eight more winners and collected four second places and ten thirds. Since place and show (second and third) finishes pay the horse owners money too, Julie Krone's popularity among the trainers began to rise.

Still, a racetrack is as much a place of dirt and sweat and danger as it is a place of dreams. Even winners have to prove themselves over again each day. Julie Krone went about the business of proving herself with as much determination as any rider had ever mustered, but on some days she must have wondered if it would be enough. Racing fans, called railbirds for the way they seem to perch on the rail that runs along the track, would shout, "Hey, sweetheart, why don't you go on home and have babies?" Too many owners would dismiss her from consideration because she was a female, never mind how often she won. The male jockeys resented her, bad-mouthed her, and harassed her.

Pressures like that might help explain what happened at Bowie Race Track in Maryland in 1981. Though within a year she would become the first woman to lead a meeting at a major track (Atlantic City) in winners, the 1981 meeting at Bowie was mostly hard times for Julie Krone. She'd developed a tough shell, but she was still only seventeen. She was a long way from home, and most of the folks with whom she spent her days wished she'd go away. She'd tried marijuana as a kid when she was mad at her mother and father for getting divorced and madder at her classmates for laughing at her or ignoring her. She tried it again at Bowie, and this time she got caught. She was suspended from racing for two months. With nothing better to do during the suspension, she walked to the track each day at dawn and watched the morning workouts through the fence. She was so miserable that she made a vow. Never again would she give anyone any reason to deprive her of the opportunity to ride horses fast for a living.

But when she returned from the suspension, things got even

worse for Julie Krone. Initially nobody wanted to hire her, which was an old problem. Then, when she finally did get a chance to ride at Laurel Race Track in Maryland, her mount threw her and she broke her back in the fall. Recovery meant two months in bed — pure torture for somebody as active as Julie had always been.

Four months after the accident, she finally worked her way back to the track, only to encounter the horror that all athletes most dread: the slump. No matter whom she rode for, no matter how fast the horse, she couldn't win a race. Her bad mounts ran true to form, and her good ones stumbled or bolted or tired. Eighty times she left the starting gate without finishing first, a stretch that left her standing beside the track one afternoon screaming, "I quit! I quit! I quit! I can't stand it!"

Fortunately at least one trainer wasn't listening to her tantrum. Bud Delp hired Julie Krone to ride some of the horses in his charge, and Krone began to win again. Over the following years, by dint of her ability, her perseverance, and the fact that even men who don't believe women can ride will learn to love a winner, Julie Krone became the tenth, and then the eighth, and finally the fourth best jockey in the country. It was a level of success that no female rider had ever achieved, let alone sustained.

Which still didn't exactly make her one of the boys. The fans, at least those who bet on other jockeys, continued to yell at her to go home and wash dishes. And a lot of the men riding against her wished she'd do that, too. During the 1986 meeting at Monmouth Park in New Jersey, fellow jockey Miguel Rujano slashed Krone across the face with his whip during a race. Rujano claimed Krone was crowding his horse, but Julie wasn't buying that argument. After the race, she punched Rujano in the nose. He countered by throwing her into the jockeys' swimming pool and holding her head underwater, but she got away from him, climbed out of the pool, and hit Rujano over the head with a chair. Both jockies were fined for the incident, and Krone

apologized, at least for the part about the chair. But she also said to a reporter afterward, "Hey, this is a rough game, and you can't let yourself be a victim out on the track."

Julie Krone took her own advice to heart, but she tried to control her temper, too. It wasn't easy, because even as she began to win more races, earn more money, and attract the notice of more trainers and owners, she had to endure the harassment of folks for whom ability and hard work meant little against the power of old prejudices. The fact of Krone's success, the courage she'd demonstrated in her riding, and the resilience and determination she'd exhibited in coming back from her injuries were nothing to some of the horse owners and racing fans. They still didn't consider her business women's work.

Her colleagues continued to be a problem, too. When their horses lost to Julie's, they couldn't shake the notion that they'd been beaten by a girl, and they didn't like it. In February of 1988, by which time Krone had won more races than any woman in history, she faced another dramatic challenge from a fellow jockey. She was passing a horse ridden by Armando Marquez in the homestretch when Marquez reached over and yanked the reins out of her hands. Had Krone fallen, she might have been badly hurt, or even killed. She had the broken back to remind her of how serious a racetrack spill could be. But Krone, reaching back for the horsemanship — or horsepersonship — she'd been cultivating since the age of two, managed somehow to stay aboard her mount and finish second in the race. Marquez was disqualified for his flagrant foul, and Krone was declared the winner. But more important, she managed to restrain herself from hitting the culprit in the nose or banging him over the head with a chair. The combination of superb riding and remarkable self-control seemed to argue that Julie Krone might be on the brink of even more spectacular success.

Of course the only place where success is certain is in the movies. The real world of charging horses and tight turns usually finds a way to ditch the script. A little later in 1988, racing this time at Aqueduct in New York, Julie Krone fell from her mount. Her shoulder was badly damaged when the horse landed on her, and the bruises she sustained made it impossible for her to move for three days.

Still, she finished the year as the country's ninth-leading rider and had every reason to look forward to an even bigger year in 1989. Except that in a race at the Meadowlands in November, she took another, even more frightening spill. "My horse just dropped," she said later. "I hung on to the reins with my left hand as I went tumbling over his head, and he pulled my arm right out of the socket." Two other jockeys went down in the same spill, and one of them, Richie Migliore, broke his neck.

That accident took Julie Krone out of horse racing for eight and a half months. It also left her with a four-inch steel plate and seven screws in her left arm and shoulder, which meant, as one sports columnist put it, that for the first time in her life she probably weighed more than one hundred pounds.

She came back again, of course, though she chose to ride at a track outside the New York–New Jersey area. When she was asked why, she said, "Well, if you wrecked the same car three times, wouldn't you sell it?"

Soon enough, though, she was back at the biggest tracks, racing against the best and most famous jockeys. Where once she had had to plead for a few mounts a week, now she was setting records. She rode four winners in one day at Aqueduct. Then, to prove it was no fluke, she won five races in one day at the Meadowlands and six in one day at Monmouth Park. Most jockeys are delighted with two wins in an afternoon. Finally, in the summer of 1992, she became the first female jockey to win a season's title at a major racetrack, totaling seventy-three winners at Belmont Park.

As a little girl, she had ridden for pure joy, the only pure joy she could find. As an experienced jockey, she has married that joy to a fierce work ethic, and she has learned, as all successful athletes must, how to endure and prevail. She learned to trade in the flamboyance of the little girl who used to stand up in the saddle and sing for the steadiness the everyday rider must achieve. When someone asked her how she could ride at all after the fall that had crushed her shoulder, she shrugged and smiled. "Sometimes I have to use both hands where I used to use one," she said.

But one thing has never changed. Julie Krone on a horse has been leaving the doubters slack-jawed and shaking their heads since she was two. Linda McBurney, an exercise rider who quit racing after twenty starts, perhaps put it most succinctly when she addressed the question of whether her friend Julie Krone had made it easier for other female riders who want to be taken seriously at their work. "She has cut a path through the deepest, darkest jungle," McBurney says. "But she cut it so fast and so clean that it closed off behind her."

Edson Arantes do Nascimento ("Pelé")

Perhaps the greatest compliment that can be paid an athlete is to say he or she changed his or her game. Babe Ruth changed the way fans thought about home runs. Bobby Orr redefined every hockey fan's understanding of the defenseman's role. And then there was Pelé. He made soccer his personal stage. He imagined impossibly intricate moves — crazy, acrobatic dances of scoring. He showed players and fans that soccer could be in the present and the future at the same time, on the same field.

I have an extra instinct for the game. Sometimes I can take the ball and no one can foresee any danger. And then, two or three seconds later, there is a goal. This doesn't make me proud, it makes me humble, because it is a talent that God gave me.

— *Edson Arantes do Nascimento*
("Pelé")

ONE AFTERNOON late in the summer of 1950, in a small Brazilian town called Bauru, a nine-year-old boy named Edson Arantes do Nascimento got his heart broken. As he listened on a static-choked radio, Brazil's soccer team lost the World Cup final to Uruguay.

Edson, whose father was the veteran soccer professional Dondinho do Nascimento, couldn't believe his beloved Brazilian team had lost. Meanwhile his mother, Celeste, couldn't believe that she was seeing that stupid game undo another member of her family. As the boy cried and his father hung his head, Celeste shouted at her husband, "Do you see what soccer has done? It has made you suffer, and now it is making your son suffer."

Dondinho had no reply. How could he argue? His pursuit of the opportunity to play pro soccer had not only led him to forsake other, steadier work; it had once injured him so badly that for a time he could do no work at all. The family had always been poor, as had their neighbors in Bauru. In order to play soccer at all, Edson or one of his friends had to steal a sock from somebody so that they could fill it with rags or maybe other socks and use it as a ball. Many of the boys had no shoes to wear on or off the soccer field, which led neighborhood jokers to call their team "the barefooted ones." As far as Celeste do Nascimento was concerned, her husband's crazy love for soccer was largely responsible for their poverty and the cruel jokes at her son's expense. And now the game had made the boy miserable.

Only the ability to see into the future could have given Dondinho a retort to his wife's angry accusations. Then he would have known that in the 1958 World Cup tournament, the very boy now crying in front of the radio would lead the Brazilian team to the first of its astonishing three World Cup championships. Of course by then the entire soccer-playing world would know Edson Arantes do Nascimento simply as Pelé.

Even in the age of televised sports, when every imaginable athletic event is beamed into homes across the United States from around the globe, it is difficult for many U.S. citizens to understand the international significance of the World Cup Soccer Tournament. For millions of people in scores of countries, it is the Super Bowl times ten. It is a World Series that really does determine the champion of the world, rather than only the best team in North America. And since the tournament occurs only once every four years, it is preceded by a level of anticipation that fans in the United States, with their bloated and overlapping sports seasons, cannot really comprehend.

Pelé's own first experience under the global spotlight of the World Cup tournament was the stuff of dreams. From the days of kicking the tightly rolled socks on a dirt field, he had progressed through a series of better and better amateur teams. Time and practice sharpened his skills, and the skills carried him to games on bright, well-tended fields surrounded by hundreds, and then thousands, and then tens of thousands of fans. Pelé once said, "I came from nothing," yet in spite of the grim poverty of his beginnings, the climb seemed somehow natural and easy. Once, looking back, the established champion said, "I knew how to play soccer on the street, without shoes, without a professional ball, without a uniform. When I moved on to a very comfortable field covered with beautiful grass, why wouldn't I win? I had to win." His success on the soccer field even won over his mother, who cheered with the rest of the growing crowd and celebrated with the family at home.

Natural though it may have felt to Pelé himself, his rise through

soccer's ranks in Brazil was meteoric. Pelé — the origin of the nickname is not known — was only seventeen when he was picked for the national team, the club that would represent the country in the World Cup tournament in 1958. He was the youngest player in the entire tournament, and he was perhaps the most excited. But from the start, his excitement was tempered by anxiety. He'd been kicked in the knee in a game earlier in the season, and he was not at full strength. Whenever he ran hard, the knee throbbed and distracted him. A knee injury had ended his father's career, and Pelé was haunted by fears that he, too, would never get the chance to fulfill what appeared to be his enormous potential. Maybe he wouldn't be able to show the world how well he could play. Maybe he wouldn't be able to play at all.

That was the nature of the pressure that weighed on this boy of seventeen on the day the Brazilian team visited the country's president, Juscelino Kubitschek de Oliveira. It was a few days before the team's departure for Sweden, where the World Cup tournament would be held. Kubitschek de Oliveira had heard of Pelé's achievements as a player, and he singled the teenager out during the ceremony, shaking his hand and saying, "I am very happy to meet you, Pelé. I see this is the new Brazil."

Lots of athletes have been invited to visit with presidents and senators, or kings and queens, but these visits usually occur after the athlete has *won* something. Presidents and kings know that a little basking in the reflected limelight of a champion will enhance their own popularity. But what was this teenager with a bad knee to make of the fact that the leader of his nation was telling him he was "the new Brazil" before he'd even warmed up for game one? Pelé began to long for the day that the games would begin. At least on the field he had always felt comfortable.

But when the team reached Sweden and began to practice, there was no comfort for Pelé. After each session his knee was swollen and sore. Several times he went to the coach and asked to be sent back to Brazil. Perhaps an able-bodied player could replace him, someone who might better serve the team. The coach urged Pelé to be patient, to let his knee heal. Then he placed his young player on the reserve team for Brazil's first game, a match with the Austrian team. Pelé was at once relieved and frustrated.

Pelé watched and rested as Brazil beat Austria and then played to a scoreless tie with England. It was the lack of offense in the game against the English team that led the coach to insert Pelé's name in the starting lineup against Brazil's next opponent, the team from the Soviet Union. For though he had developed a complete game in his rise from the dirt playgrounds to the glamour of the World Cup, it was his marvelous knack for breaking away from the opposition and finding a way to put the ball into the net that distinguished Pelé's play. Soccer is a game in which the scoring of a goal can be a rare event. Most matches are low scoring, and many end in scoreless ties. But the quick and inventive Pelé was a threat to score from any place on the field.

Although he did not score in the game against the Soviet Union, a 1–0 win for Brazil, Pelé impressed everyone who saw him that day. In fact, he so impressed Brazil's next opponent, the French team, that when that match began it was immediately evident the French players were trying to slow down Brazil's young star. After scoring within the first few minutes, the French players began roughing up the Brazilians, particularly Pelé, hoping to intimidate them, to keep them off balance, and perhaps to discourage them from pursuing the ball as aggressively as they'd have to in order to win.

While the game was still young, Pelé, who was already limping and bruised, surprised himself and his teammates by delivering an impromptu pep talk. He doesn't remember what he said, but the pep talk worked on at least one player: Pelé himself. He scored three goals that day, leading Brazil to a 5–2 comeback victory and the opportunity to meet the team from Wales in the semifinal match.

By the day of the game against Wales, Pelé's fame had spread around the globe. Nobody scores three goals in a World Cup match and stays anonymous. Pelé's achievement might be compared to hitting five home runs in a World Series game or passing for eight touchdowns in the Rose Bowl. And Pelé gave his fans something more to cheer about when he scored the only goal that day with a play the equal of which even the most experienced soccer fans had never seen. With his back to a defender, Pelé lobbed a kick over his own head. The ball bounced off the body of one of the Welsh players, and before it could touch the ground, Pelé spun into position and rapped the ball sharply past the bewildered goalie. Later people would call the beginning of that remarkable move "the bicycle kick" because of the way Pelé seemed to spin like a wheel in knocking the ball over his own head. On that day they just called it genius.

By whatever name, the remarkable acrobatic feat catapulted the Brazilian team into the finals, where the Swedish team would be the opponent. Sweden scored the first goal that day, and the hometown crowd shouted its encouragement, but the joy was only temporary. Ten minutes into the second half, with the outcome of the game still in doubt, Pelé took a pass in front of the Swedish goal, dribbled the ball like a juggler on his instep for a second, and then suddenly flicked it over the goalie's head and into the net to put his team in front, 3–1. The two teams traded goals over the remaining minutes and then, as time ran out and the realization dawned on everyone that this particular World Cup tournament was destined to be the Pelé Show, the Brazilian magician took center stage once more. Pelé took a teammate's high pass deep in the offensive zone, caught the ball on his thigh, and in the same motion turned, popped it into the air, and headed it past the goalie into the net.

Pelé and his teammates threw their arms around each other and shouted with joy. Even the Swedish crowd had to acknowledge that they had seen something special that day: the emergence of soccer's greatest star.

Back in Bauru, Dondinho do Nascimento finally had his reply. "Yes," he could say to his wife, Celeste, "soccer can make you suffer. But see what else it can do? See how it can bring you joy?"

Throughout Brazil, people danced in the streets, triumphant at the country's first World Cup championship. There was no precedent for their excitement, and the celebrating would go on for months. When they returned from Sweden, Pelé and his teammates were flown from city to city, and everywhere they were wined, dined, and cheered. In writing his biography of Pelé, James Haskins said, "Every night the players had to remove flowers and confetti from their hair and clothes and massage their cheeks, sore from so much smiling."

The problem with conquering the world when you are only seventeen is that when you get up the next morning, you have to find something else to do. Pelé managed that challenge better than many young champions have. He continued to excel as a member of the Santos Soccer Club in Brazil, leading the team to triumphs at home and abroad. His play was so consistently spectacular that teams from France and Spain tried to buy him from the Santos owner, but the owner laughed at these offers. "Pelé is not for sale," he said, "and besides, if I did sell him, the people of Brazil would lynch me!"

Still, in the same mystical way in which athletes like Babe Ruth and Muhammad Ali have transcended mere sports and the boundaries of nations, Pelé was becoming an international treasure and a citizen of the world. In France they called him *la Tulipe Noire* (the Black Tulip); in Chile he was known as *el Peligro* (the Dangerous One); in Italy they knew him as *il Re* (the King); and at home in Brazil, his fans began to call him *el Pérola Negra* (the Black Pearl).

Scientists began wondering how to explain Pelé's unprecedented performances. How was he able to move so quickly? to change directions so effortlessly? to decide with such uncanny insight what his opponents would do next, then beat them to the open spot on the field or pass the ball to a teammate who had been left alone when the defense scrambled to cover the explosive Pelé? Their tests revealed that Pelé's peripheral vision was 30 percent greater than that of the average athlete, which partly explained how he could see and understand so much of what was happening around him on the field. They found that his heart rate was much slower than the rate of most athletes, and that he could recover from physical effort much more quickly than the average soccer player.

Some writers tried to use these findings to demonstrate that Pelé was a freak, a superman whose success had resulted from genetic advantages. But those who had paid attention to Pelé's career from its beginnings in the street outside his tiny home knew that much of his magic was the result of hard work. Most of the moves with which he had astonished huge crowds around the world he had practiced for hundreds of hours. Nobody had played more soccer than Pelé. Nor did he do all his work on the athletic field. This reluctant student who had never progressed beyond the fourth grade read many histories of soccer and studied geometry and chess. Each new way to understand an angle, which could be translated into the way an opponent might think or a soccer ball might bounce, might provide another advantage he could use in a game.

The 1962 World Cup tournament, the first after Brazil's triumph in Sweden, took place in Chile. To nobody's great surprise, Pelé led his team through the tournament and into the finals. And in the championship game against Mexico, he scored the goal that gave his country a 2–1 triumph.

Pelé's success in those back-to-back championships lifted his popularity still higher. Brazil actually passed a law that prohibited the Santos team from trading him out of the country. On an international level, too, he was larger than life. Some years later, when the Biafran war was raging in Nigeria, Pelé visited the country for an exhibition match. For the sake of seeing Pelé play, the two warring sides managed to suspend the fighting. Pelé played in Nigeria one day, and when the game was over, an officer in the Nigerian Army ferried him halfway across the river that separated the two combatants. A Biafran army officer took custody of Pelé in the middle of the river and escorted him to a field on his side, where Pelé played in a second game. The next day he departed, the interlude of sanity passed, and the Nigerians and Biafrans returned to the mad business of war.

Even the greatest stars sometimes fail, of course, and four years later, in the 1966 World Cup tournament, the Brazilian team failed utterly. The English team won the championship, which was decided on their shores. Pelé was so badly fouled, so frequently tripped, tackled, and kicked throughout the tournament that he vowed he would never again play World Cup soccer. Disappointed fans accused their former hero of being lazy, and some even attributed Brazil's failure to win the Cup for a third consecutive time to Pelé's marriage, which had occurred earlier in the year. They felt he had perhaps become too fat and happy to lead his team to victory again, though no man from any country had ever played on three World Cup champions.

In any case, Pelé finally could not resist the challenge to play in another World Cup competition, and he agreed to lead his Brazilian team into the 1970 tournament in Mexico. It was his fourth such adventure, he was nearly thirty, and he must have felt as if he'd been playing forever. Once the tournament's youngest player, he was now among the oldest, and not everyone was convinced that he still belonged. Some Brazilian fans even booed as he took the field for the first of the team's matches. They felt that he'd been shown up four years earlier at the 1966 World Cup games and that whatever magic he'd once possessed was gone.

But Pelé proved to them that he had one more glorious race to run. He averaged a goal a game during the six matches of the qualifying round, and when Brazil reached the finals, it was Pelé who headed in the goal that put the team ahead to stay against runner-up Italy. When that day was done, Brazil had won the World Cup for the third time. No team had done it before, and no team has done it since.

When Pelé announced his retirement from international soccer four years later, the numbers he left behind were extraordinary. In 1,254 regular season games, he had scored 1,220 goals — nearly a goal per match in a game known for stingy defenses. He had led the Santos team to numerous championships and international acclaim. He had helped Brazil retire the World Cup trophy: the team had won the greatest of soccer prizes three times and earned the right to display the Cup at home forever. But perhaps more important than these achievements was the extent to which Pelé had captured the imagination of the world with his brilliant and creative play. Even in countries like the United States, where soccer was a poor second cousin to baseball, basketball, American football, and hockey, Pelé had become a tremendous attraction. When the Santos team played exhibition games in the U.S., it regularly drew enormous crowds. People who'd never seen a top-flight soccer game before, folks much more familiar with the talents of Willie Mays or Wilt Chamberlin or Bobby Orr, would walk away from those games swearing that Pelé was the most wondrous athlete they'd ever seen.

So it was no surprise when, in 1976, the New York Cosmos, a mediocre but wealthy team in the fledgling North American Professional Soccer League, lured Pelé out of retirement for one final turn in the spotlight. He was thirty-five and past his prime, but the team's owners hoped that Pelé's magic and the luster of his name would fill their soccer stadium, and that once people had seen the game, they'd enjoy it enough to return.

As long as Pelé played for the Cosmos, the strategy seemed to be working. His club regularly outdrew all the other teams in the league, and for a time it looked as if Pelé would single-handedly bring the United States into the community of nations crazy about his game. During his three years as a member of the Cosmos, Pelé helped lead the team to its first North American Soccer League championship. But it turned out that for North Americans, Pelé was bigger than the game itself. A few years after he retired, the Cosmos and the whole league of pro soccer teams collapsed.

The game Pelé played so brilliantly gave him a great deal in return, and he has taken advantage of his opportunities. Soccer introduced him to the international community, and Pelé learned to speak four languages in addition to his native Portuguese. This boy who "came from nothing," as he once said about himself, became wealthy enough to have homes in Santos, Rio de Janeiro, and New York.

But the rewards have not come without cost. The spotlight that fame brings is bound to cast shadows. Before the 1970 World Cup final, many members of the Brazilian team had been concerned that the generals who had assumed power in their country would use the triumph of Brazil's soccer team to increase their own popularity and solidify their despotic control. Pelé would not join his teammates in condemning the generals. "You cannot not play because the government is not good," he said, and many observers accused him of naïveté and worse. Some ridiculed him as a puppet of the generals. But Pelé had always devoted himself to the game and to the joy it could bring its fans. "If we win," he told his teammates, "there are still problems, but at least the people get happy for some months."

Pelé was true to that elemental philosophy when he invited homeless people to live rent-free in the real estate he'd bought in Brazil thirty years ago. He remained true to it when the Pepsi-Cola Company gave him hundreds of thousands of dollars to represent their products. "I won't take your money for going to cocktail parties," he

Joan Benoit Samuelson

It is true that all records fall, and the ones Joan Benoit Samuelson set in the Boston Marathon in 1983 and the 1984 Olympic Marathon will be no exception. But long after her numbers have been eclipsed, people who saw her run will talk about her fierce and steady determination and her astonishing resilience. And then someone will remember that she wanted to call her autobiography *Out on a Limp,* and everybody will laugh. And somebody else will say, "You know, there never was a more delightful champion." And everyone will agree, because that will be true, too.

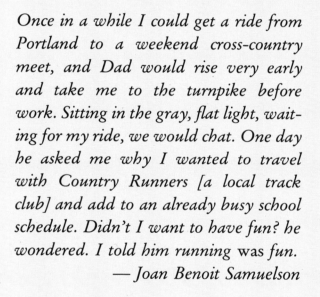

Once in a while I could get a ride from Portland to a weekend cross-country meet, and Dad would rise very early and take me to the turnpike before work. Sitting in the gray, flat light, waiting for my ride, we would chat. One day he asked me why I wanted to travel with Country Runners [a local track club] and add to an already busy school schedule. Didn't I want to have fun? he wondered. I told him running was fun.

— Joan Benoit Samuelson

MARCH IS NOT Maine's best season. Spring never comes early to northern New England, and the wind off the ocean in March stings a runner's cheek. But that discomfort was nothing compared to the pleasure of running near home, and so Joan Benoit was training in Cape Elizabeth, minutes from her family, in the middle of the March preceding the 1984 Summer Olympics.

There were other advantages to Cape Elizabeth. Though the roads and paths there are not free of traffic, there is still farmland to see. The view of the sea is fine, if you don't mind the solitude. And Joan Benoit knew all the routes up there so well that she was unlikely to be surprised or distracted from the business at hand. At one time she'd tried to keep to untraveled roads because running competitively had seemed so preposterous to her. As a schoolgirl she first discovered the joy running could bring her. It was all hers, and all she had to do to improve was run more. Her shyness was no handicap. Maybe it was even an advantage. She ran alone and loved it. But she was embarrassed about declaring herself a marathoner, saying it to the world by training seriously where anyone might notice. When cars would pass her in those days, she would sometimes stop running and pretend she was picking flowers. But now the solitude was simply one useful component to the concentration Joan Benoit had built to complement the joy. She'd acquired an iron sense of purpose that had been wearing

down opponents for ten years, and that would drive Benoit through another decade of championship performances.

The run started off well. Why should it have been otherwise? Joan Benoit was the country's best female distance runner. She'd won the Boston Marathon twice, the second time the previous April (1983) in a world record time: 2 hours, 22 minutes, 43 seconds. She'd won major marathons in Eugene, Oregon, and in New Zealand as well, and too many shorter races to count. At least *she* hadn't counted them. And now, in the best shape of her career, she was pointing for the Olympic Trials, which were less than two months away. She'd picked the twenty-mile loop in Cape Elizabeth that day because it was a run that had always provided her with a sense of how well her training was going. She expected good news.

But with three miles to go, she felt an unfamiliar sensation in her knee. Later she would say it seemed as if "a spring were unraveling in the joint." She tried to run for another two miles, but the knee complained too loudly. When she could no longer stride, she hobbled. When she could no longer hobble, she walked.

"Injuries are part of the game." Maybe this is the most familiar cliché in all of sports. But each particular injury is new and ominous when it happens, and this one had picked a heck of a time to occur. Nearly every girl and boy who has ever run or jumped well enough to dream about excelling at it has entertained fantasies about the Olympics. Now here was Joan Benoit on the brink of the glorious realization of that fantasy. All she had to do was gradually bring her training to the peak she had learned to achieve for her biggest races and finish among the top three U.S. women in the marathon portion of the trials, which would be held in Washington State in May.

But you don't get to run in the Olympics if you don't qualify in the trials. And you don't run in the trials on a knee that feels like somebody's working on it with pliers.

"This was the most frightening moment of my life," Benoit said several years later in *Running Tide,* the autobiography she wrote with Sally Baker.

It was no exaggeration. Since childhood, Benoit had pushed herself to excel, first as a skier, then as a field hockey player, and finally as a runner. As a little girl, she had skied into the darkness of early evening rather than quit the slopes before she absolutely had to do it. A frostbitten fingertip was a small price to pay for the additional run or two that might make her more competitive. Once she'd begun running seriously, she'd always driven herself harder than any coach would. "I liked pushing myself to keep going after exhaustion set in," she has said. "It was a game I played."

Always the point of the game was to be as good as she could possibly be at what she was doing, and always that goal seemed to be just beyond the next marathon, the next ten-kilometer run, the next workout. Setting that sort of goal is a private way of motivating oneself, a way that lots of people might not understand. Winning races, especially races as famous as the Boston Marathon, might seem to be achievement enough to the people lining the course and clapping as the runners rush by, but winning has been almost incidental to Benoit. Even as a freshman at Bowdoin College she was uncomfortable with the praise she gained as an outstanding field hockey player. "I would squirm under the compliments," she remembers, "not in false modesty, but because I had a voice inside that said, 'Watch it.' I knew I was capable of more, and that kept me honest."

Even Joan Benoit's closest friends — the ones who best understood her determination and her enormous capacity to endure the rigors of long-distance running — were worried in the spring of 1984. The fluky injury was followed by weeks of indecision. Some days the knee felt fine. On other days it hurt just to walk upstairs, and that was when participation in the Olympic Trials couldn't have seemed more impossible. The most frustrating part of the ordeal was that the doctors Benoit consulted kept advising rest, the one suggestion she couldn't take seriously. Who could rest? When in the past had rest ever helped her prepare for a race? She'd always said, "Mileage is my safety blanket. I feel I'm doing okay if I put in enough miles. And if I don't burn off my energy every day, I'm disoriented and grumpy." She was not likely to sit back and watch cartoons on T.V., even if that was what the doctor ordered. She was far more inclined to say, "When in doubt, run harder," and in her case "harder" meant more than the usual 100 to 120 miles each week.

March dragged into April, and the knee did not improve. In fact it seemed to be getting worse. Normally the doctors might have performed an arthroscopy, a procedure in which they insert a tiny scope into the knee and examine it to see if a ligament or cartilage has been torn. But with the Olympic Trials only weeks away, they were reluctant to do it. People recover from arthroscopy much more quickly than they do from more major knee surgery, but no surgery is truly minor. Even if they could diagnose and correct the problem with the arthroscope, the trauma of the surgery and the training time lost to it would certainly cost Benoit her shot at the Olympics.

To make matters even more improbably dramatic, the 1984 Olympics were particularly special for a number of reasons. The U.S. had boycotted the previous Games in 1980 to protest the presence of troops from the Soviet Union in Afghanistan. Hundreds of athletes, Joan Benoit included, had been denied the opportunity to participate in the spectacle by politics. Nobody, least of all Joan Benoit, wanted to be denied again. Beyond that, the 1984 Olympics were to be held in Los Angeles, so there would be an opportunity for U.S. athletes to perform before their countrymen and countrywomen. And finally the '84 Olympics would provide women with their first opportunity to run the marathon in the Games.

Under the curious assumption that females were somehow incapable of running twenty-six miles, the Olympic Committee had always limited them to shorter races. Even the growing popularity of marathoning among women and the triumphs of Benoit and other champions such as Ingrid Kristiansen, Rosa Mota, Grete Waitz, and Charlotte Teske hadn't earned female marathoners a chance to run in the Olympics until 1984. Now the opportunity was at hand, and there was serious doubt about whether the very best of all the American women runners would be able to compete.

Joan Benoit underwent arthroscopic surgery three weeks before the trials. Dr. Stan James found a fibrous mass called a plica that had become inflamed and was interfering with the normal movement of the knee joint. He removed it. Benoit awoke from the anesthetic and, still groggy, called a friend to ask if she could pick Joan up on her way home from work and take her running. It was a notion so goofy that even Benoit can't quite believe she ever had it.

Still, she was swimming and riding a stationary bicycle within days of her release from the hospital, and running again within a week. Drawing on her own determination and the support of her family and friends, she resumed her training, overcame a pulled hamstring muscle that resulted from favoring the knee, and appeared for the Olympic Trials as scheduled.

"Even as I was jogging to the starting line, I honestly didn't know if I could manage the race," she remembered afterward. She told her family not to come to the trials because she feared that she'd run badly if she ran at all. But when race day came, her brother and his wife were there. They claimed, transparently, that it was just one stop on a West Coast trip they'd been meaning to take anyway. Benoit admitted later that having them there had never been more important.

She ran conservatively that day and was surprised at the relative ease with which she covered the first twenty miles. The years of training and discipline seemed to carry her along automatically for a while. But with six miles to go, her legs suddenly remembered all the miles

they'd missed over the past two months. The knee, only three weeks out from under the surgeon's scope, turned cranky. Benoit began concentrating on planting her feet with each stride to spare the joint unnecessary wobbling. She ran more and more slowly, more deliberately, less naturally, and although the commentators kept saying she was looking good, she knew otherwise. She kept sneaking peeks over her shoulder, wondering why some of the other runners were not moving up on her. That nobody did was a measure of her dominance of the U.S. marathoners.

Even as she crossed the finish line first, though, Joan Benoit was figuring that it would be different in the Olympics.

Perhaps it was partly doubt that drove her to train so effectively in the days between the trials and the Olympic Marathon itself. When that race finally came, it crushed other champions. The weather was so hot and miserably humid that Grete Waitz, one of the prerace favorites, later said, "I could have run faster, but I was afraid of dying." She was hardly overstating the case. Switzerland's Gabriela Anderson-Schiess was so dehydrated by the time she reached the finish line that she was disoriented and staggering.

Amid that drama, Joan Benoit was the picture of superb efficiency. This time she never looked back. A photograph taken during the race says it all. It shows Benoit running past a building upon which there is a huge mural that depicts her victory a year earlier in the 1983 Boston Marathon. Also in the photograph is Bill Rodgers, the great marathoner whom Benoit had idolized as a young woman. He is perched on the back of the pace truck, providing television commentary for the race. The photograph is splendidly full of meaning. Joan Benoit is running alone, of course, since she ran most of the race alone. (She led it wire to wire.) But it also seems to symbolize the way in which she consistently ran beyond her own previous triumphs. The win in Boston depicted in the mural established a world record, but the central figure in this picture is not dreaming of a past victory; she is churning toward the next. And it is the man, Rodgers, who watches and talks about it, as the woman, Benoit, runs into history.

The Olympic course in Los Angeles ended in the Coliseum, an enormous stadium packed with fans from all over the world. In order to enter the stadium that day, Benoit ran through a tunnel. She was alone, and she knew she had won. She remembers thinking, "Once you leave this tunnel, your life will be changed forever," and she remembers that then she fastened her eyes on her shoes and turned her attention back to maintaining her pace. She concentrated on only that until she had crossed the finish line. Then she raised her arms over her head and ran a victory lap around the Coliseum, waving at the applauding crowd. Her smile was glorious, exalting, and grateful all at once.

Her life did change, as the lives of Olympic gold medal winners are likely to do. But it changed less than the lives of other winners who have not been so firmly grounded in values more substantial than winning. When she was asked where she could be found after the Games, Joan Benoit said, "Look for me in a berry patch in Maine." She was not entirely successful at keeping her distance from the clatter and clamor that inevitably follow a triumph as large and public as hers had been, but within a short while she had reestablished the calm that had always seemed to lie at the center of her running life and her life beyond running. Even under pressure from those who were competing for her attention, offering her endorsement opportunities, or merely calling to wish her well, she remained the quiet, somewhat shy young woman from Maine.

Shortly after the 1984 Olympics, Joan Benoit married Scott Samuelson. The following years brought them two children, Abigail and Anders. In 1991, Joan Benoit Samuelson acknowledged that taking care of the kids was like running a ten-kilometer race each day, but she has managed to train and race competitively nevertheless. If two operations on her heels, a bad knee, a bad back, and various other aches and pains couldn't slow her down, why should two kids?

Even before the children were born, Joan Benoit Samuelson talked about the challenge of balancing her passion to excel as a runner with the other demands of her life. In her autobiography she says, "Winning is neither everything nor the only thing. It is one of many things." It's a concise statement of a truth that has eluded so many athletes, so many coaches, so many fans. It's a perspective that has not only granted Joan Benoit Samuelson the awareness that nobody runs forever but also has enabled her to recognize, sometimes to the surprise of folks accustomed to dealing with single-minded, self-centered athletes, various concerns other than winning in the small context of a game. When she was invited to the White House to meet President Carter, she discussed the dangers of nuclear power; when she visited New Zealand, she marveled at the extent to which people there have avoided the pollution that chokes the American cities in which she has run; when she needed a way to explain her discomfort with those who would celebrate her, she had the wit to transcend her own literal experience and find an aphorism that author Elie Wiesel attributes to Rebbe Pinhas of Koretz: "If someone finds it necessary to honor me, that means that he is more humble than I. Which means that he is better and saintlier than I. Which means that I should honor him. But then, why is he honoring me?"

It is an intriguing question, and one that not many runners or jumpers or ballplayers think to raise. It speaks to the heart of the tension between the illusion of heroic stature and the plain fact of human foolishness and fallibility, a tension that many athletes ignore or deny. That she should cite it hints at the perspective Joan Benoit Samuelson has brought to balancing her furious drive to compete and win with the apparently equally powerful urge to give of herself to others and the recognition that life outside and beyond her running is large and various. She has been injured enough to wonder whether the next injury will prevent her from running for pleasure in five years or ten, when her competitive days are done. But this possibility, too, she faces with calm good humor and the recognition that she cannot know everything. She'll know an answer when it comes. In her autobiography she wrote, "Every step I take pushes me further into the mystery." She has been challenged to remember that she is only herself, even as the world has celebrated her and roared for curtain calls. "Look for me in a berry patch in Maine," she has responded with a smile. Until the next race begins.

Nate "Tiny" Archibald

A lot of the men who played on the same teams as Nate "Tiny" Archibald will tell you that he never said much. That's a peculiar quality in a game much given to woofing, trash-talking, and one-upsmanship by mouth, but Tiny never seemed to have time for that segment of basketball. He was too busy cutting by men who were ten inches taller than he was, or stealing the ball, or popping it in from thirty feet as the buzzer sounded. And even when the season was over there was no leisure for talk. Because then it was time to go back to the playgrounds and teach the game to everyone who was willing to work all day long to learn it.

Once they make it, they're gone. Once they get the big car, they point it out of here. Except for Tiny. He came back.
— *Hilton Barker,*
community worker in the
South Bronx, New York

LIKE COUNTLESS CITY KIDS, Tiny Archibald grew up dreaming of playing pro basketball. It's a low-percentage dream. There are so few jobs in the National Basketball Association, and so many hungry applicants. Even boys who grow up in ghettos where the schools are third rate have a far better chance to become doctors or lawyers than they do to compete in the NBA. And even the ones who make it to the pros often have careers that last only a few years.

But the logic of numbers couldn't compete with the glamour of the dream for the young Archibald, who early on inherited the nickname "Tiny" from his father. Tiny wanted to play the game he loved against the very best. And he coupled his dream with a dedication that few of his fellow ballplayers could match. Even his mother was astonished by Tiny's determination and by the way it drove his concentration on the game. "It's just as though he was in a cave, and all that was in the cave was a basketball and a hoop," she told John Devaney, who wrote a book about Tiny years later.

In his cave, Tiny was focused and safe. As a little boy in the South Bronx, he played basketball each day after school. If the gym was open, he played indoors as long as there were ten guys there to make up two teams. After everybody else went home, Tiny stayed around and popped jump shots by himself until the janitor told him it was time to lock up. Then he went outside and fired away at the basket on the asphalt court outside. The rim was bent and somebody had stolen the net, but it was still a basket. Tiny would practice until it

was too dark to see whether his shots were going in or not. Then he'd dribble the ball he'd borrowed from the coach all the way home. He'd practice dribbling behind his back and between his legs, moves that required concentration enough so that he didn't have to notice the garbage and wrecked cars in the streets. With a basketball in his hands, he could pretend not to hear the youngsters who were calling to him to come over and share the wine they were drinking or the drugs they wanted him to try. The street life of the South Bronx had no place in Tiny Archibald's cave.

Early in his high school career, though, there came a point where dedication to basketball and an insatiable appetite to practice the game seemed to have carried Archibald as far as they could. He came home from school one evening to learn that his father had departed the premises, which meant that even the spotty income he'd been providing was gone. There wasn't much room for economizing. Already Tiny and his three brothers were crowded into one room. His mother and Tiny's three sisters shared the other one.

Tiny had never been much of a student, and when his father deserted the family, the little interest Tiny'd had in academics vanished entirely. At the end of the semester, he'd flunked so many courses that he was no longer eligible to play basketball. When he learned that he'd lose his spot on the team until his grades improved, he went to his coach, Floyd Lane, and told him he was quitting.

"What? Because of the grades?" Lane asked. "Don't be a jerk. Hit the books. Get the grades back up. There'll be a place for you when you do."

"Nah," Tiny told him. "I'm quittin' school, too. I gotta find a job, help support my family."

Floyd Lane had heard that song before, but it broke his heart to hear it from Tiny. "What are you gonna do?" he barked. "Wait tables? You gonna wash dishes?"

"Whatever I can find," Tiny said with a shrug.

"I'll tell you what you can find," Lane said. "You can find a whole lot better job if you pay attention to what you gotta do here at school, then get yourself back on this basketball team. We'll get some college coaches in here lookin' you fellas over, handing out some scholarships, and you won't be here to show 'em what you can do if you're elbow deep in suds somewhere."

"I don't know . . ." Tiny muttered.

"Listen to me," Lane demanded. "You remember the day you first tried out for the team?"

"Me and about nine thousand other guys, all of 'em good players." Tiny smiled.

"Sure," said Lane. "And I told you to drive to the basket, show me how you drive, and you did, and I said it was all wrong."

"Yeah," Tiny said. "You said I was out of control."

"And you did it again, and again after that. And I said, 'No! No! No!' And the next thing I know, you're gone right out of the building."

"I almost didn't come back," Tiny said.

"But you *did* come back, didn't you? And then you remember that day that summer I had those fellas from the Knicks in here? You didn't much like that, either."

"I couldn't see how I'd ever play against guys like that," Tiny said. "I could play against the best on the playgrounds, but those guys looked like they were ten feet tall."

"And you wondered what all you were workin' at then, didn't you? And I told you then. And I'm tellin' you again now. Maybe you'll make it to the NBA, and maybe you won't. It's not impossible. There's fellas six foot or so, just like you, who have made it before. But you leave this team and this school, you won't make it ever. And if you stay, if you tough this out, you may get a chance to go to college on a basketball scholarship. You take advantage of that, and even if you don't ever play a day as a pro, you'll have *something*.

You'll have a college degree. And you'll have a better job than dishwasher and a lot more ways to help your family, too."

Tiny Archibald had never been much of a talker, but that day, fortunately for him, he was a good listener. He took Floyd Lane's advice. He survived a semester without basketball and improved his grades. Then he rejoined the team. And when Don Haskins, then the basketball coach at Texas Western University (now the University of Texas at El Paso) stopped by to see whether his old pal Floyd Lane had any players worth recruiting, Tiny Archibald was the one who caught his eye.

Because he never grew to be taller than six feet one, Tiny Archibald should have been at a serious disadvantage in a game dominated by giant centers and wide-body forwards — a game in which even the guards were often six four or six five. But he compensated by developing the ability to make everyone on his team a better player. This is a curious talent shared by some of basketball's best players: the Isiah Thomases, Larry Birds, and Magic Johnsons. Their passes are so precise they make the players who catch them look as if they are exactly where they are supposed to be. They expect so much from their teammates that their teammates find themselves delivering more than they knew they had. Tiny Archibald made himself that kind of player in college at Texas Western University. Perhaps because he'd worked for all those hours in the gym and on the playgrounds at home, he discovered that he had developed the remarkable knack of doing whatever his team needed done. He could score when he had to, and led his conference in scoring. But he could get the ball to his teammates as well as any guard in the country, and he ran the team with confidence and imagination.

Bob Cousy, formerly a brilliant guard with the Celtics and coach of the Cincinnati Royals during Tiny's senior year in college, had heard plenty about the Texas Western guard. Though he'd never seen

Tiny play, Cousy chose him in the second round of the 1970 NBA draft. A few weeks after the draft, Coach Cousy was in New York on business and called Tiny, who was visiting his family in the Bronx. How would Tiny like to stop by Cousy's hotel room so the coach could get a look at him?

"Sure," Tiny said.

A while later Cousy heard a knock at his door. When he opened it, his jaw dropped a foot. "Geez," he told his coaching staff when he'd returned to Cincinnati, "I knew he was little, but I didn't know he was *that* little. Or that skinny. Or that baby-faced. I thought he was the bellhop."

Bob Cousy wasn't the only man who had trouble believing Tiny Archibald really belonged in the NBA, at least at the outset. The first time Tiny's team came into New York's Madison Square Garden to play the Knicks, Tiny didn't arrive with his teammates. He'd stopped off to visit his brothers and sisters, and he came downtown to the Garden by himself. The usher at the players' gate wouldn't let him in, figuring he was just a teenager trying to see the game for free.

"I play for the Royals, sir," Tiny told him, but the guard just smiled. "Sure, kid. And I'm the shortstop for the Yankees."

Eventually Tiny got the guard to call Coach Cousy in the locker room, or he might have missed his first chance to play in front of folks from his hometown. "Yeah, he's one of my guys," Cousy told the astonished guard, "but I don't blame you for wondering about it. We haven't even got a uniform that fits him yet. His number's stuffed halfway down into his pants."

Tiny Archibald's first few years in the NBA were remarkable on a number of counts. Bob Cousy asked him to "quarterback" the team in his rookie season, and he did the job so well that many were surprised when Tiny was left off the All-Star team. During his second season he *was* an All-Star, though the Royals did not accomplish much as a team. The club's move to Kansas City–Omaha didn't improve it either, but Tiny kept soaring. During the 1972–73 season, he became the only player ever to lead the NBA in both scoring and assists, averaging thirty-four points and eleven assists per game. That year the *Sporting News* voted him Pro Basketball Player of the Year.

During those heady times, lots of things changed for Tiny. He had money to help his family, just as Floyd Lane had predicted he would one day. And it was a good thing. Two of Tiny's brothers had begun using drugs. He sent them money to come to Kansas City and join him, figuring that they'd never make it if they stayed in the South Bronx. Meanwhile Tiny himself commuted back to New York each spring, as soon as the NBA season was over. "I think every black man who gets out of the ghetto has an obligation to the kids on the block," he told those who wondered why he never took the summers off. He set up playground leagues and funded clinics. He brought NBA players into New York for exhibitions. He sponsored tournaments and set up educational programs. Of the kids he was trying to help he simply said, "If I can get them playing basketball all day, all they're going to feel like doing at night is going home and sleeping."

Two years later, Tiny led the Kings to their first playoff appearance, and though the team lost early in the so-called "second season," Tiny was proud of the progress the Kings had made. But NBA basketball, like all the professional sports, is a business without much room for loyalty or sentiment. Before the 1976–77 season, Tiny was traded to the New York Nets. A year later he was playing for Buffalo, and a year after that a multiplayer deal took him to the Boston Celtics. None of the three teams were enjoying good seasons in those years, and Tiny Archibald began to wonder if he'd ever experience the thrill of playing for a champion. He'd set records, played in several All-Star games, and been voted Player of the Year, but he'd never helped his team to an NBA championship. In fact, he'd never been close.

His chance came in the 1980–81 season. That year the Celtics, a team that had fallen apart in the late seventies, flanked Tiny with Larry Bird, Robert Parish, and rookie star Kevin McHale. Coach Bill Fitch convinced this group that it could be a contender, and during the regular season the Celts won sixty-two of their eighty-two games. At thirty-two, which is past middle age for an NBA player, Tiny was reborn. He'd lost large parts of two previous years to injuries, but this time around he not only made the All-Star team for the sixth time but he was voted the game's most valuable player. Now there were no more awards to win — save a championship ring — and as the playoffs began, Tiny Archibald found himself concentrating on that goal so hard it hurt.

Tiny scored twenty-seven points and assisted on seven more buckets against the Chicago Bulls in game one of the opening round. The Bulls never recovered. In round two, the Celtics met the Philadelphia 76ers, the club that had knocked them from the playoffs the previous year. The 76ers shocked Boston by winning two of the first three games of the series, and game four nearly ended Tiny Archibald's championship hopes. Down two points with eight seconds to go in the game, Archibald got control of a loose ball but elected not to call time-out. Instead he pushed the ball upcourt and made a bad pass, which Bobby Jones of the 76ers intercepted. With one play that he'd have given anything to call back, Tiny had handed Philadelphia a three-games-to-one advantage — a lead that a team that good was almost impossibly unlikely to lose. If the 76ers finished Boston off with one more win, it wouldn't matter that Tiny had turned in a great season, or that he'd been the MVP in the All-Star game. This time around he'd be remembered as the goat who tossed away the playoffs with a bad decision and a worse pass.

But the Celtics came back. Tiny and his teammates whittled his goat's horns to nothing. In game five Archibald popped in twenty-three points and earned seven assists. With the game still in doubt in the closing seconds, he made the three-point play that clinched a 111–

109 win. In game six he calmly sunk two foul shots to put the Celts ahead to stay at 96–95. Game seven ended with a single point separating the two teams, but it was the Celtics who'd won.

Six games later, in a series that couldn't help but be anticlimactic, Boston had dumped the Houston Rockets for the NBA championship, and Tiny Archibald had his ring. The only person in Boston happier than Archibald himself might have been his wife. "He finally has his championship," she said with visible relief. "That's all he's talked about. Now we can get our lives together."

If Tiny's life came together then, it almost came apart a few years later when his NBA career ended. Leaving the game is tough for any pro athlete, and for Tiny Archibald it was agonizing. At first he had no idea how to fill all the hours that basketball had demanded of him since his childhood. "I'd been playing and practicing so long that I didn't know anything else," he told *Sports Illustrated*'s Franz Lidz. "I almost never came out of that twilight." The off-season wasn't the problem, of course. In the summer, Tiny could pull on his cutoff shorts, lace up his high-tops, and shoot hoops with the playground kids. Wherever his NBA career had taken him, his support for the programs he'd begun in Harlem had never waned. But what would he do when the pro basketball season began?

It turned out that he just had to look a little harder for more folks to help. And his search led him in an unlikely direction. In high school and college, Tiny had characterized himself as an athlete rather than a scholar, but at Texas Western he'd begun to think that teaching might be something he'd be good at. Now, without the grind of basketball to interfere with academics, Tiny decided to pursue that possibility more formally. He enrolled in a master's program in adult education and human resource development at Fordham University, and he liked the atmosphere of higher education so much that he eventually began work in a Ph.D. program in the same field.

Then, perhaps because the plight of the homeless in New York

and elsewhere was so much in the news at the time, it occurred to Tiny that maybe the kids on the playground weren't the only ones who could benefit from his encouragement and his example. He signed on as the recreation director for the Harlem Armory Shelter. He began calling businesses and corporations, urging and cajoling them to donate money and equipment to the shelter. Tiny wouldn't call the work a big deal. "I'm just trying to save people from the streets that I was saved from by basketball," he has said. And he had some fun at his work. One night he convinced the New Jersey Nets to part with half a dozen tickets, which he gave to six residents of the shelter. After making sure they were all wearing coats and ties, Tiny drove the men to the game and brought them into the locker room to meet the Nets. One of the players pulled Tiny aside and asked him, "Who are they? Lawyers?"

Eventually, within a few years of his retirement, the transition was complete. Tiny Archibald, All-Star point guard and playground legend, had become Nathaniel ("Nate," "Tiny") Archibald, recreation director, doctoral candidate, Harlem schools drug counselor, all-around friend to those who need one most.

In 1991, Tiny Archibald was elected to membership in the Basketball Hall of Fame. That honor insured his achievements as a basketball player would be preserved for future fans to appreciate. But Archibald's work in the schools and the shelters of New York has insured that admiration for him won't be limited to basketball fans. Those fortunate enough to have seen him play will remember him as a quick, canny, hard-working guard. Those fortunate enough to have known him will remember him as a warm, unselfish, and giving man.

Susan Butcher

There is a considerable cash prize —
$50,000 or more — for winning the
Iditarod Trail Sled Dog Race held in Alaska
each winter. The money is no doubt what
draws many mushers to endure long days
and nights of hunger, thirst, frostbite,
hallucinations, and loneliness, not to
mention the odd moose attack. But not
Susan Butcher: she probably does it for fun.

I knew if I went north I'd hit some really good stuff. People don't go where it's cold. I wanted to live someplace where I could run my dogs for hundreds of miles.

— Susan Butcher

FOR SUSAN BUTCHER, it was a day like any other: brutally cold, windy, and snowing hard enough so that it was impossible to see more than a few feet in front of the heavy four-wheel vehicle her sled dogs were dragging for practice. In short, as far as she was concerned, everything was perfect.

Then suddenly Butcher's lead dog went "gee" (right) when Butcher shouted "Haw!" (left), and the four-wheeler, the dogs, and Butcher plunged off a twelve-foot cliff and into a clump of alder trees.

There was, of course, no path out. The trail Butcher and the dogs had fallen from was little traveled, and she figured it might be several days before somebody happened by. She had no saw and no ax. It was only supposed to be a little training run. With pliers, a wrench, and a broken screwdriver, she chopped at the alders. She got the dogs working together, and they pulled the four-wheeler up the hill. Sometimes they'd make as little as twelve inches of progress before Butcher would have to begin hacking away with her pliers and wrench again, but five hours after they'd fallen, Butcher and her dogs were on the road back to her cabin. Butcher had learned not to leave home, even for practice, without all her tools. And she hoped her lead dog had learned that "Haw!" meant "Haw!"

On that day when she and her team fell off the trail, Susan Butcher was training herself and her dogs for the Iditarod, the annual sled dog race that covers the eleven hundred miles between Anchorage and Nome, Alaska. Over the years, Butcher's consistently excellent finishes in this most grueling of athletic events have become the stuff of legend, and some of the tales of her training runs are no less dramatic than the races themselves. In a funny way, Butcher's preparation for the Iditarod began before the race ever existed. When she finally entered it for the first time in 1978, Butcher must have felt like she'd finally discovered where she belonged.

As a little girl growing up in Cambridge, Massachusetts, Susan Butcher only knew where she did *not* belong. She hated the congestion of the busy streets, the constant noise of the traffic, and the pollution all around her. She begged her parents to move to the country, or at least to let her live in a tent in the backyard. Her best friends were the dogs she kept. In first grade she wrote an essay entitled "I Hate Cities." That was the first, last, and only sentence in the paper.

When she was finally old enough to leave home, she put Cambridge behind her in favor of Colorado. When the Rockies no longer seemed sufficiently remote, she headed for Alaska. She finally settled in a town called Eureka, which you will not find on many maps. There she cobbled together four one-room cabins, a doorless outhouse, and 120 doghouses. Butcher's dogs have outnumbered the two-legged citizens of Eureka by as many as 150 to 13.

Eureka is a fine place to prepare for the Iditarod, since a chief feature of both is isolation. A pitcher who's gone to a full count on the batter with the bases loaded in the ninth inning of a tie game might feel lonely. A marathoner who has run beyond whatever certainty her training can provide and still has miles to go might feel that way, too. But the Iditarod exists primarily as a tribute to the conviction that everybody ought to be able to take care of himself or herself with the help of a dozen or so dogs, and there is perhaps no loneliness like the loneliness of someone lost and snow-blind in the middle of Alaska.

A very fast and disciplined dog team with an experienced and fortunate musher can complete the race in a little over eleven days. Some competitors take as long as three weeks, and a lot of starters, as high as 30 or 40 percent some years, quit. Leaders and losers alike spend hours and hours alone and cold in a blasted white landscape. When their dog teams are traveling up a hill, the mushers run along behind them or kick with first one numb foot, then the other. When the teams are traveling downhill, the mushers hold on for their lives and pray that the wind won't freeze their eyes shut or tear the sled from their hands, leaving them without even the company of their dogs. For as long as they can stand it, they swerve over frozen rivers, navigate through the stumps of burned-over forests by the insanely inadequate glow of a single small headlight, and hope they won't suddenly crash headlong into a bear or a moose or the dog team of some poor fool who has become completely confused and started racing backward on the trail.

All these obstacles appeal to Susan Butcher, who's felt since early childhood that taking heat, light, and shelter for granted was missing the point. Only when she has felt close to nature's essentials has she felt challenged. And only when she has felt challenged has she felt entirely alive.

Joe Redington invented the Iditarod in 1973. He'd always loved the wilderness, particularly the Alaskan wilderness, and he was worried that what he loved was falling into the hands of snowmobilers and settlers with satellite dishes. He scratched his head and wondered how to remind everybody of the toughness and independence that Alaska had always demanded of its residents, and he came up with a race that would require sled drivers and their dogs to brave screaming winds, blinding blizzards, hunger, lack of sleep, and a dozen other hardships that most athletes would just as soon consider only from a great distance. He called the race the Iditarod after an Alaskan ghost town bearing the name, which is an old Indian word meaning distant place.

As an incentive to take up this crazy challenge, Redington offered $50,000 to the winner of the first Iditarod, though when the race started he didn't have the money. Twenty days later, when that first race ended, Joe had the dough. He'd hustled it from various individual and corporate donors. But over the years the payoff for winning the Iditarod continued to be a little on the shaky side. Winners have sometimes had to settle for their prizes in installments, unlike all the professional baseball, basketball, and football players who are secure in their guaranteed contracts.

Joe Redington first met Susan Butcher a few years after he'd come up with the Iditarod, and right away he was sure she'd win it one day. Or he was almost sure. He proposed a sled dog trek to the summit of Alaska's Denali, also known as Mount McKinley, perhaps partly to test the mettle of this remarkable young woman who'd come to the far north in search of escape from cars, buildings, and too many people. Together with seven dogs and a sled, Butcher and Redington made the 20,320-foot climb through hundred-mile-an-hour winds and over 2,000-foot-deep crevasses. It took them forty-four days. Nobody'd mushed that route before. Nobody's done it since. When they were finished, Redington was *absolutely* sure Susan Butcher would one day win the Iditarod.

But the extent to which Ms. Butcher fulfilled his prophesy must have surprised even Redington himself. Perhaps it shouldn't have. By the time she began to pile up first-place finishes in the Iditarod and other races in the late eighties, Susan Butcher had paid her dues. She'd learned from her limping pups to line up several friends year-round to help her knit booties for race days. Run out of booties on the trail, and the ice would cut the best team's paws to hamburger. She'd learned how to recognize a potential lead dog in a litter and how to raise all the dogs in her team to have confidence in her. And perhaps most important, she'd learned that her loyalty and attention to the needs of her canine partners would sometimes be rewarded by the special gifts the dogs had to give.

Eight years before she ever won an Iditarod, Butcher was mushing perhaps her best lead dog ever, Tekla, and fourteen other huskies

across a frozen river in a practice run when suddenly Tekla began pulling hard to the right. Butcher kept tugging on the team to follow the trail, but Tekla wouldn't respond. Though she'd never balked before, the dog insisted on pulling the sled off the trail to the right. Butcher finally shrugged and decided to follow Tekla's lead. A moment after she'd made that decision and left the track, the whole trail itself sank into the river. "She [Tekla] had a sixth sense that saved our lives," Butcher told Sonja Steptoe of *Sports Illustrated* years later. "That day I learned that the wilderness is their domain. The dogs know more about it than I do, and I'm better off trusting their instincts."

Of course instinct is only part of it. Courage, stamina, and a cool head help, too. In 1985, with a superb team and high expectations, Susan Butcher seemed to be on her way to winning the Iditarod for the first time. But she ran into a problem no measure of preparation or instinct could have forestalled. Veering around a sharp bend in the trail one night, she was startled to find in the beam of her headlight a full-grown female moose. The dog team hit the animal before Butcher knew the moose was there. By the time Butcher could figure out what had happened, the moose was hopelessly entangled in the harnesses that connected the dogs. In the carnage that followed, two of Butcher's dogs were kicked to death and several others were badly injured. While Butcher fought to free the remaining dogs from their harnesses, the moose stomped on her shoulder and might have killed her, too, if another musher hadn't arrived on the scene and shot the moose. Butcher and her team limped to the next checkpoint and resigned from that Iditarod in the low point of her racing career.

And then, beginning in 1986, the high points began coming in quick succession. Between 1986 and 1990, she won the Iditarod four times. The hottest selling T-shirt in the state bore the legend "Alaska: Where Men Are Men and Women Win the Iditarod." After Butcher's third win in a row in 1988, Joe Redington laughed and told a reporter,

"It's getting pretty damn hard for a man to win anything anymore. Maybe we should start a race especially for them."

It has been suggested that the formula for winning the Iditarod involves having good dogs, a good musher, and good luck — in about equal measure. The good musher is the one who can smile into the wrath of an unexpected hundred-mile-per-hour wind, but he or she better make sure the smile is behind several layers of ski mask, because when that wind joins below-zero temperatures, a smile will freeze on the lips for hours, and maybe forever. Susan Butcher proved she could brave the most vicious weather, but by the time she started winning the Iditarod, she'd learned to prepare herself and her dogs so well that all but the most hideous storms seemed routine. She'd also learned that by working closely with her dogs every day from the hour they were born, she could build a level of trust and loyalty that her competitors could only envy. Of course, this relationship demanded a good deal from Butcher, too. In 1991, she passed up the chance to win her fifth Iditarod when she decided that a blizzard raging over the last hundred miles of the course would unreasonably endanger her team. She prolonged a rest stop, waiting for the weather to improve, and finished second that year.

Even when the blizzards hold off and the moose stay out of the way, the Iditarod demands a tremendous amount from a musher. The rules require one mandatory rest period of twenty-four hours during the race, and once having met that requirement, no serious competitor stops for more than four hours at a time. Nearly all of the four hours of each stop are taken up by feeding the dogs, melting snow so they'll have water, checking their paws for cuts or cracks, mending the harnesses, and maybe catching something to eat — hot chocolate if you're fortunate enough to be stopping at a checkpoint where somebody's cooking, melted snow if you're not.

That doesn't leave much time for sleep, so the Iditarod's exhausted competitors have been known to hallucinate on the trail. In a book entitled *Woodsong,* a musher named Gary Paulsen wrote of a fellow who appeared on his sled wearing horn-rimmed glasses, clutching a stack of important-looking papers. "He is the most boring human being I have ever met," Paulsen says in his diary-like account. "He speaks in a low voice about federal educational grants and he goes on and on until at last I yell at him to shut up. The dogs stop and look back at me and of course I am alone."

Though Susan Butcher also might well be susceptible to hallucinations, her dogs probably know her too well to be surprised by anything she could say or do. Certainly she knows them well enough to astonish her friends. "Folks ask how I can call one hundred and fifty of them by name," she says, "but it's natural. They're like children. If you had one hundred and fifty kids, you'd know all their names, wouldn't you?"

Becoming the world's most successful musher and one of the very few sled dog drivers capable of making a living at the sport has never turned Susan Butcher's head, though it has gone some way toward fulfilling her dream. "I never got into this to make a lot of money," she told an interviewer before winning her fourth Iditarod, in 1990. "But to live just the way you want, to do what you love to do. . . . How could you have any complaints?"

Still, success at the Iditarod *has* changed Susan Butcher, if only a little. Before she became a celebrity, at least by Alaskan standards, she used to go off and live alone for six months or so. No people, no running water, no nothing. Now, in deference to the fact that people want to contact her and because raising and training 150 dogs takes the sort of money only sponsors can provide, she has a phone in her cabin. She has a husband there, too. His name is David Monson, and as a matter of fact the phone was probably his idea. He serves as Susan Butcher's business manager, and he probably got pretty tired of hitching up the dogs and mushing more than twenty miles every time he had to make a call.

Which is not to suggest that David Monson is exactly a softy. He got to know his future wife when they were both unknown mushers competing in the 1981 Iditarod. Monson was struggling to climb a hill and lost control of his sled, which wound up off the trail in the brush. It was the same stretch of brush Susan Butcher had already fallen into a few minutes earlier, and while they were both working to straighten out their dog teams, a third musher also skidded off the trail and landed on them. Monson remembers it as chaos: forty-five dogs and three mushers, including a very angry and competitive woman and one guy (Monson) who didn't really have much idea what he was up to. When they all finally got back on the trail, Butcher told Monson he'd better rest his dog team, and that was the last he saw of her in the race. If it wasn't love at first sight, it was close enough for the two mushers, now partners as well as competitors.

Not all the others who tackle the Iditarod have been as comfortable with Susan Butcher's triumphs in the race as David Monson has been. Rick Swenson, the only person to have won the race as often as Butcher has, tried for some years to get the Iditarod's organizers to adopt a handicapping system that would, in effect, penalize Butcher and other women racers for weighing less than the men who mush against them. When that didn't work, Swenson took to intimating that Butcher won only because she had a lead dog of supernatural strength and endurance, an unintentional compliment, since Butcher had raised and trained the dog. Butcher herself tends to shrug off the bitterness of the men who resent a woman's success in a sport they'd like to claim as their own. "Yes, I am a woman," she told writer Carolyn Coman in an interview for the book *Body and Soul.* "Yes, it is a victory for me to win the Iditarod. But it isn't amazing that I, a woman, did it. I did it because I am capable, and women are capable."

Being capable may never before have involved such an effort. Butcher has said on several occasions that training for the Iditarod — which involves raising, feeding, running, and training her dogs as well

as keeping herself in shape — is an eleven-month proposition. Small wonder that sometimes she thinks about turning her attention exclusively to some of Alaska's shorter races — the three-, four-, or five-hundred-mile jaunts. She already knows these races well. She holds the records in most of them, just as she does for the Iditarod. So easing up a little is a pleasant possibility that occupies Susan Butcher sometimes when she thinks about a post-Iditarod future.

Unhappily, there's an unpleasant possibility that concerns her, too. She has adjusted to the modern improvements David Monson has made in their cabin, but other adjustments won't come so easily to the woman who hated the noise and pollution and hustle of Cambridge when she was a little girl. The authorities have begun to improve the roads up Susan Butcher's way, and Butcher has watched "progress" suspiciously. "In ten years we may have ten or fifteen neighbors," she was overheard to say. "If that happens, we'll be gone."

Muhammad Ali

Boxing has always been full of hype and hot
air. Every championship match is billed as
the fight of the century. Every new
heavyweight finds himself portrayed as
granite-jawed and unstoppable. Crooks
and mobsters and light-fingered managers
have corrupted boxing . . . always.
But Muhammad Ali brought his sport into
the consciousness of people who'd never
paid it any attention before. He even
won over folks who hated his profession, and
he compelled them to care about the
sport and about him. He made boxing glow
for a time, and when he left it, the
lights over the ring went out.

I'm a perfect role-model for children; I'm good-looking, clean-living, cultured, and modest.

— Cassius Clay, 1963

Why do they want me to be in this film? What did I do to be with all those great people?

— Muhammad Ali, 1990,

after being invited to participate in a documentary to follow Eyes on the Prize, *a series about the civil rights movement featuring James Meredith, Rosa Parks, and Martin Luther King*

BIBBITY-BIBBITY-BIBBITY-BIBBITY-BAP! bap! bap! bap!"

In a corner of the Miami gym, the slender young heavyweight drilled the speed bag. Veterans of the fight game and tourists alike marveled at the quickness of his hands.

"Who is he?" asked one.

"Why, that's Cassius Clay," said another. "He won a gold medal in the Olympics in 1960."

"He's beautiful," the first said, and that was true. The fighter's face was unmarked and classically handsome. He said it himself all the time.

"Who's he gonna fight?"

"He's fighting Sonny Liston for the heavyweight championship of the world," the fight fan said.

"Oh, dear," came the reply. "What a terrible shame."

When Cassius Clay, later and ever after known as Muhammad Ali, stepped into the ring on the evening of February 25, 1964, 93 percent of the sportswriters in attendance expected him to be nothing more than a footnote to the violent career of Sonny Liston when the night was done. At best, they figured he'd be a *noisy* footnote. Clay had seen to *that* at the weigh-in, the prefight ceremony which requires each fighter to step on a scale and had never before amounted to much else. This time it was different. Cassius Clay, the twenty-two-year-old challenger, had entered the room screaming, "I am the champ!

I'm ready to rumble! Round eight to prove I'm great! Bring that big ugly bear on!"

Nobody at the weigh-in had ever seen anything like it. More than one writer was convinced that young Clay was crazy, and the physician in attendance figured the fighter was scared to death. Some wondered if Clay would even show up for the actual bout. But a few say now that they saw him wink, and realized even then that Clay was putting on a show.

It was nothing to the show he would put on when the bell rang. Through the first two rounds Clay danced, frustrating Liston, who could not catch up to him to hit him. In the third round the attack began, and Clay opened up a gash under Liston's right eye. Observers at ringside looked at each other in disbelief. When had any of them ever seen the invincible Liston cut before? And when had his own attempts to hit an opponent been so futile? He looked as if he were trying to catch the wind.

But this fight would not be a simple matter of youth versus age or speed versus power. Toward the end of round four, Clay suddenly started having trouble with his eyes. When the round was over he returned to his corner shouting that something was stinging them. "I can't see," he screamed to his trainer, Angelo Dundee. "Cut the gloves off! We're going home!"

But Dundee wasn't quite willing to go along. What the heck . . . his guy seemed to be winning the fight. Maybe he could do something for the eyes. He wiped them with a sponge, dried them, rinsed them out again. When the bell rang to begin round five, Clay's eyes were still tearing. But Dundee shoved the fighter's mouthpiece back in, stood him up, and shouted, "This is the big one, daddy. Stay away from him. Run!"

Clay "ran" for about a minute and a half of round five, and then his eyes cleared. Whatever had been stinging him — maybe something Liston's handlers had been putting on his cuts — was gone. In round six Clay tattooed the champion at will, and Liston couldn't touch him. When the bell rang to start the seventh round, Liston wouldn't answer it. Later he said he'd injured his shoulder and could no longer fight. In any case and against all odds, Cassius Clay was now the heavyweight champion of the world.

Even larger surprises followed. At a press conference the day after the Liston fight, the new champion told reporters, "I know where I'm going and I know the truth, and I don't have to be what you want me to be. I'm free to be what I want."

In that moment, sports fans became aware of the ongoing transformation of Cassius Clay into Muhammad Ali, the man who would not only set the world of boxing on its ear by winning the heavyweight championship two more times, but who would also outrage the American establishment and eventually charm millions of people all over the globe.

Nobody could have seen all that coming in 1964, though hindsight helps make sense of Muhammad Ali's remarkable journey. As a boy growing up in Louisville, Kentucky, he'd assimilated the system of racial segregation that nearly everyone in the American South then took for granted. He'd heard and never forgotten the story of Emmett Till, a black youngster murdered by white men in Mississippi for whistling at a white woman. In 1960 he'd returned with a gold medal from the Olympics in Rome to find that there were still places in his hometown where he could not eat lunch because he was black, albeit an American champion. And eventually, during the early sixties, he'd found a faith to help him understand and stand up to these conditions. The speech the new heavyweight champion made to the press after he'd beaten Sonny Liston was the beginning of Muhammad Ali's declaration of his allegiance to the Nation of Islam, a religion headed in the United States at that time by Elijah Muhammad.

Elijah Muhammad referred to white people as "devils" who had enslaved black Americans for centuries and were still doing so. Muhammad Ali never entirely accepted this characterization, but sportswriters and others were outraged by the new champion's association with the Nation of Islam. His kindest critics called him a fool.

On May 25, 1965, the young champion gave Sonny Liston the customary rematch in Lewiston, Maine. The fight went down in history as the one you missed if you blinked. Muhammad Ali knocked out Sonny Liston in the first round, before many of those who'd come to watch the bout had taken their seats.

For the next two years, Ali defended his championship against all comers. He beat Floyd Patterson in the United States, George Chuvalo in Canada, and Henry Cooper in England, among others. But during those years another opponent was emerging, and this would be one even Ali could not knock out. Throughout the decade of the 1960s, the United States had been sending soldiers to Southeast Asia to fight in a war in Vietnam. Some of the young men who fought in the war went voluntarily, because they felt it was their duty to serve when their country was involved in a war. But many of the American soldiers in Vietnam were drafted, and many of the draftees were black and poor. Elijah Muhammad, among others, felt this was completely unjust. Why should young black men fight for a country that discriminated against them? Muhammad Ali agreed, and when the United States Government tried to force him to serve in the army, he told them, "I ain't got no quarrel with the Viet Cong." In a quieter moment later on, he referred to his work as a minister in the Muslim faith, the faith embraced by the Nation of Islam. "My faith prohibits me from fighting in the war," Ali contended, "just as it requires me to pray five times a day. How can I kill somebody when I pray five times a day for peace?"

The government didn't see the contradiction, and although there was a provision in the law allowing for the release from military service of young men whose consciences or religious convictions made going to war impossible for them, Muhammad Ali was brought to trial for refusing to join the army. Almost immediately he was stripped of the heavyweight championship and prohibited from boxing. He would be banned from the ring for three and a half years, until the United States Supreme Court could finally reverse the conviction. In other words, Muhammad Ali was denied the opportunity to box until one court could rule that another court, as well as every boxing commission across the country, had been wrong.

Boxing is a terrible way to make a living. Almost nobody who boxes for long comes away from it without eye damage, ear damage, kidney damage, or brain damage. But the attraction of the sport for those who follow it is the purity of courage at its center. Many of the people who promote the fights may be liars and crooks, but once the bell has rung, the contest between two fighters gives each the opportunity to test his strength, his endurance, and his nerve. Muhammad Ali had never lacked any of these qualities in the ring, but now circumstances forced him to find another kind of courage. If he'd agreed to go into the army, he would almost certainly have been safe from harm. As a celebrity, the heavyweight champion, he'd have traveled from military base to military base entertaining the troops with boxing exhibitions. Perhaps he'd have been asked to speak publicly in support of the war. Probably he'd have been free to continue earning his living in the ring. But Muhammad Ali chose the more difficult alternative, the alternative of conscience, and he paid the price for that choice.

By the time Ali was allowed to return to the ring in 1970, a great many people in the United States had decided for a great many reasons that the war in Vietnam was wrong. Many hundreds of thousands had marched in Washington to protest the continuation of the war. And Muhammad Ali himself had become for many folks, black and white, a hero, a fellow who'd shown others how to stand up for themselves and their beliefs.

Back in the ring, he went about trying to do what such great

heavyweights as Jack Johnson and Joe Louis had never managed to do: to regain the championship title. His first opportunity to do so came against Joe Frazier, a powerful and relentless puncher. The two met on March 8, 1971, in New York's Madison Square Garden. They hammered each other for fifteen rounds, and in the end the judges declared Frazier the winner. Observers of the fight saw with dismay that during the three and a half years away from the ring Ali had lost a good deal of his foot speed. He could still punch, as indicated by Frazier's battered face, but he could no longer dance away from his opponent's punches as he had once done. He could no longer escape harm as often as he had in the early years. And the longer he fought, the greater the risk of lasting damage would become. Ali must have understood this, but he gave it little thought as he recovered from the first fight with Joe Frazier and began looking ahead to his next opponent. When you lose to the champion, you have to fight your way back into contention again. It would be three years before Ali would have another opportunity to box for the title.

By 1974, heavyweight boxing, largely through the efforts and charisma of Muhammad Ali, had become a strikingly glamorous affair. Movie stars and other celebrities regularly attended the fights. Closed-circuit theater broadcasts had made it possible for fighters to earn five million dollars in a night. But according to boxing folks in the know, no amount of money should have been enough to induce the aging Muhammad Ali to fight George Foreman, the reigning champion. Not only had Foreman beaten Joe Frazier, he had hammered and dazed him so thoroughly that the fight had to be stopped in the second round. And George Foreman had knocked out nearly everyone else he'd ever fought, too. Like Ali, he'd won an Olympic gold medal — but he'd won it eight years more recently than Ali. Their battle in Zaire, the so-called "Rumble in the Jungle," had all the makings of a terrible mismatch.

And when the fight began, that was what it looked like. During the first round, Ali danced as he had in the old days, but it was obvious he couldn't do it for long. Angelo Dundee and the others in Ali's corner only hoped he could somehow stay away from young Foreman long enough to tire him out. Then maybe Ali would be able to wear him down further with punches. Maybe there'd be a chance. But the first part of the plan had to be "Dance for as long as you can."

Imagine the horror in Dundee's heart, then, when Ali stopped dancing toward the end of round one and leaned passively against the ropes. He watched as Foreman hesitated, then started throwing punches. Here was a heavyweight's dream: an apparently stationary target. Foreman launched an enormous left hook that would have ended the fight if it had connected, but it missed by six inches. He launched another one, and it missed, too. Dundee prayed for the bell to ring. It finally did, and each fighter returned to his corner.

"What are you doing?!" Dundee and the other corner men screamed at Ali. "Get off the ropes! Don't let him tee off on you that way! He'll kill you!"

Ali looked at them serenely, weirdly composed in the middle of the noise and excitement. He'd been fighting professionally for fourteen years, and he'd had hundreds of amateur bouts before he'd turned pro. He knew as well as anyone alive how alone a boxer is in the ring. A thousand people can shout advice. Ten million can cheer for you or roar for the other guy to knock your block off. But finally you find your own way in the ring, and Ali felt he'd intuitively discovered the way to beat the heavily favored Foreman.

For the next six rounds, eighteen eternal minutes, Ali kept backing onto the ropes and covering up his face with his hands. Foreman obligingly trudged after him, banging away at Ali's sides, his shoulders, his arms — any target Ali would present.

"What's happening?" somebody shouted at Dundee.

"I don't know," the trainer had to admit. He'd never seen anything like it. Ali seemed to be inviting the champion to beat him to pieces.

But suddenly, in the seventh round, Foreman began to appear exhausted. Norman Mailer, one of the writers attending the fight, later described him as looking like he was trying to climb a mountain of pillows. By round eight he had nothing left. Ali waited for him to throw a punch that would expose his head, and then, as if he'd been planning it for months, he knocked Foreman out.

Later that night it rained hard, the way it rains only in the tropics. A reporter named Pete Bonventre decided to try to visit the cottage where Muhammad Ali was staying to see if he could get a post-fight comment or two. The rain had kept the other writers away, and when Bonventre finally made it to Ali's porch, he found him on the steps. "Three hours after the greatest victory of his life," the reporter recalls, "Muhammad Ali was sitting on the stoop, showing a magic trick to a group of black children. It was a rope trick, where the rope is cut in half and then it's suddenly back together again. And it was hard to tell who was having the better time, Ali or the children. All I could think was, I don't care what anyone says, there'll never be anyone like him again."

Muhammad Ali did not retire, even after reclaiming the title. As a young man he had beaten Sonny Liston, who had seemed so much stronger and tougher. As an old man, at least in boxing terms, he had beaten Foreman, who was young as Ali had once been. He went on to fight for five more years. He ignored the evidence of his own deterioration and the pleading of his fans, his family, and his doctor. He lost the title to Leon Spinks, then won it back again. Nobody had ever reclaimed the heavyweight title that many times.

But Muhammad Ali took several fearsome beatings. He began to suffer from a condition called Parkinson's syndrome. After he finally did retire, he often appeared tired and awkward, which was sad for people who had watched him dance in the ring. He often had difficulty speaking clearly, which was sad for the people who had heard him talk with such wit and fire and conviction.

Boxing damages everyone it touches, and it has damaged Muhammad Ali. But he still prays five times each day. He still travels all over the world, urging people to live in peace. And he still represents for countless people, whether they like boxing or not, an embodiment of courage.

Billie Jean King

Before Billie Jean King succeeded in doing it, no woman had ever made more than $100,000 in a year by playing tennis. Today, $100,000 is small change for many women on the tour. Of course, before Billie Jean King, there really *was* no women's tour. She agitated for it, bullied her contemporaries into joining it, found a sponsor to bankroll it, ballyhooed it all over the country, and then starred on it for as long as her knees would let her. She is the mother of contemporary women's tennis, and all contemporary female players should probably curtsy, Wimbledon-style, in her direction before each match they play.

At my funeral, nobody's going to talk about me. They're all just going to stand up and tell each other where they were on the night I beat Bobby Riggs.
— *Billie Jean King*

EVEN AS A LITTLE GIRL in the fifties, Billie Jean King looked like a bad match with tennis. Her name was Billie Jean Moffitt in those days, and she was sometimes called "Little Miss Moffitt," though she was also called by a lot of less-flattering names. The game was still private country clubs then, and she was public courts. Tennis was quiet, and Billie Jean was boisterous. Tennis looked over its horn-rimmed bifocals and down its patrician nose, and Billie Jean, resplendent in rhinestone-studded specs, grew into a teenager who whooped when she won, sometimes making more noise on the court than the politely applauding crowd in the stands. And most important, from the start Billie Jean demanded fair play from a game that presented itself as "amateur" but then slid expense money under the trophy table to a few fortunate male players.

Billie Jean's determination was evident early. At the age of five, she told her mother that she was going to do something wonderful with her life. At first she thought she might be a baseball player, and her father, a Long Beach, California, fireman, obligingly carved her a bat. He was also the one who eventually suggested that she'd have more opportunity as a tennis player. He was persuasive enough that young Billie Jean put down her bat and picked up a dime-store racquet. She would not stop swinging a tennis racquet for the next forty years and more.

Billie Jean lucked out when the town of Long Beach hired a tennis pro named Clyde Walker to travel from public park to public park, instructing whatever kids showed up. After the first circuit one summer, Walker was surprised to see the same pudgy kid with the big plastic glasses at every location.

"What are you up to?" Walker asked the girl. "I just worked with you yesterday."

"This is how I'm gonna get better," Billie Jean told him. Walker shrugged and worked with her some more.

Even in those days, Billie Jean appeared to run against the grain of tennis history. Female champions had usually been long-legged and graceful. The legendary Suzanne Lenglen was perhaps the best example. She moved so smoothly, so elegantly, that she seemed to play without effort. She waltzed through her matches.

Billie Jean, on the other hand, had legs like sausages. She churned around the court like a little truck. She had trouble breathing sometimes, due to asthma and allergies, so that her play always looked like hard work. Her vision was so bad that she had to wear thick glasses to see the ball at all. In a sport famous for its silences, she talked to herself. Except when she was yelling at herself. She didn't even dress right. As a youngster she was yanked out of a team picture because her shorts and T-shirt were deemed inappropriate attire. Her mother had to make her a tennis dress before Billie Jean could return to the team.

But nobody denied that she could play. She made it all the way to the championships at Wimbledon while she was still a teenager. Then, in 1961, in an upset that must have thoroughly surprised even its perpetrators, Billie Jean and her partner, Karen Hantze (Susman), won the women's doubles title. After the match longtime tennis writer Bud Collins congratulated Billie Jean and Karen, wishing them a good time at the celebration he was sure would follow their victory.

"What celebration?" asked Billie Jean.

"Why, you're a Wimbledon champion. You'll be toasted at the Wimbledon Ball," Collins said.

"Nah. We're going back to the hotel," Billie Jean told him. "We don't have the right clothes for a ball."

Mom wasn't there to make a dress that evening. Still, Bud Collins felt that some sort of celebration was called for. He took the two champions out for spaghetti.

A year later at the same tournament, Billie Jean beat the world's number one player, Margaret Smith (Court). The youngster was on her way to making Wimbledon her own personal showcase. Four years after beating Smith, Billie Jean beat Maria Bueno, the era's best candidate for a Suzanne Lenglen–type player, in the finals. At the end of that tense match, Billie Jean threw her racquet into the air and felt, as she remembers, "as happy as I'd ever been in my life. Finally I was Number One. In my mind I was the best player in the world." Then she returned to her hotel and found the closest thing to prize money that big-time tennis paid in those days: six Mars bars which some friends had left on her bed.

It may seem ridiculous that all anybody used to be able to win at Wimbledon was a silver plate and some candy bars, but the enormous prize money available to the great tennis players of today is relatively recent news. The Steffi Grafs and Jennifer Capriatis of the world owe the same sort of thanks to Billie Jean King that today's millionaire major league baseball players owe to mavericks like Curt Flood, who challenged the reserve clause and opened the way for free agency.

Billie Jean King taught people to take women's tennis seriously by playing hard and well, by speaking out against the tournament committees that treated women as second-class citizens, and by encouraging her fellow pros to demand fair pay. She refused to be ladylike; she never shut up. A lot of that work went on behind the scenes and earned King neither money nor publicity. But the single event more responsible than any other for catapulting King and women's tennis into the public consciousness earned her a great deal of both. That event was a tennis match that begged to be written off as a joke. It occurred on September 20, 1973, and it decided the championship of nothing. On that night, Billie Jean King, the best female player in the world, crossed racquets with Bobby Riggs, a fellow who'd last won a major tournament two years before Billie Jean's birth. King was young, fast, and strong. Riggs was old, slow, and full of baloney. On the face of it, nobody should have cared much who won. But when Ms. King snapped her first serve into Mr. Riggs's forehand, an astonishing forty million people were paying close attention.

The match was an oddity for lots of reasons beyond the unprecedented interest it drew. It was being played in the Houston Astrodome, a building designed for almost any sport but tennis. Both players worried about losing sight of the ball in the lights. Each player had agreed to a best-three-of-five-sets format, although women regularly played best-two-of-three. But perhaps the strangest thing of all about King versus Riggs was that Billie Jean King, who made a career out of seeking and overcoming challenges, had tried to avoid this particular challenge for more than two years.

Ever since anyone could remember, Bobby Riggs had been only incidentally a tennis champion. His real game was hustling other players — fooling them into thinking they could beat him so they would bet on themselves, then surprising them when the money was on the table. He'd done this as a child. He'd done it at Wimbledon in 1939, when he bet a couple of hundred dollars on himself and made thousands by winning the singles, doubles, and mixed doubles titles. Much later he would do it by offering his opponents bizarre advantages. He'd put chairs on his side of the court, or he'd play while walking a dog on a leash.

Billie Jean King, on the other hand, played the game straight and hard. What did she need with this crazy confrontation with Bobby Riggs?

The simple answer is that she felt responsible for defending the image of women's tennis, a cause to which she had been devoting herself for a dozen years. With broadsides and boycotts, King had fought the promoters who'd sometimes paid the women pro players as little as 10 percent of the prize money they were paying the men. She'd struggled to put together the women's tennis union and a tour of female professional players. In 1971, when her efforts were just beginning to succeed, Bobby Riggs had started badgering her to play him in a match that would, he said, establish once and for all that women's tennis was a second-rate sport which nobody should bother to watch. "Even an old duffer like me can beat the best the women have to offer," he crowed.

As far as King was concerned, he might have gone right on crowing into his dotage, but Riggs got lucky. Margaret Smith Court, another stalwart of women's pro tennis and a champion herself, announced that *she'd* play Riggs. They met on May 13, 1973, and Old Bobby, ever the hustler, played the fact that it was Mothers' Day for all it was worth. Before their match began, Riggs greeted Court at the net with a bouquet of flowers. She was undone, and might as well have been unstrung, as Bud Collins might say. Margaret Court never found her form that day, and with his array of drop shots and lobs, Bobby Riggs beat her, 6–2, 6–1.

"That's it. I've got to play him," said King when she heard the news. And that's how the silliest tennis match that forty million people ever watched came to be.

Because it was largely the creation of Bobby Riggs, the big night was preceded by months of publicity. Riggs toured the country telling anyone who would listen that although women were delightful, they certainly had no place in tennis. He traveled in the company of several young women who called themselves "Bobby's Bosom Buddies" and pretended to worship him. He talked tirelessly about the special vitamin diet that would enable an old has-been like himself to whip the best the female side of pro tennis could provide.

Meanwhile his opponent was trying to stay clear of the circus Riggs was producing and make a living at tennis. As the Riggs match approached, King had her own worries. At the U.S. Open in Forest Hills, New York, she became so sick she had to withdraw from her third-round match in the singles tournament. Rumors began to circulate. King had thrown the match, some said. She'd feigned illness so that she wouldn't have to play Riggs. Others said King's illness was all in her head, or that it had been brought on by some mysterious psychological power that Riggs had over her, and over women in general.

Meanwhile the evidence was mounting that the King-Riggs contest had captured the imagination of the country more than any mere national championship ever had. On the Saturday before King versus Riggs, Stanford played Penn State in the college football Game of the Week, and at halftime the Stanford band formed the letters "BJK" across the field and played the popular feminist anthem "I Am Woman" full blast. "I honest to God got teary-eyed," Billie Jean remembers.

But the hours before the match brought doubts, too. Though King had been able to shrug off the news that oddsmakers had made Bobby Riggs the betting favorite, she was dismayed to learn that most of her friends among the female pro players were betting against her. The notion that women were second-rate athletes died hard, even among some of the female athletes themselves. Then, just before heading into the Astrodome to face Riggs, Billie Jean ran into old friend Bud Collins, who'd bought her dinner after she'd won her first Wimbledon title twelve years earlier and had been a close friend ever since.

"How'd you bet?" Billie Jean asked Collins.

"I went with Bobby," he said.

Terrific, she thought. She had confidence in herself, but what if everybody else knew something she didn't?

At the appointed hour, Riggs entered the Astrodome in a rickshaw drawn by his entourage of women. He was apparently having the time of his life. King made her entrance on a litter covered with feathers. Several male bearers carried her shoulder-high. She smiled and waved, even though she had always been uncomfortable with even modest heights.

Once they'd reached the court, Riggs presented King with a big, lollypop-type candy called a Sugar Daddy. Unlike Margaret Smith Court, King was ready for Riggs in the psyche department. She gave him a piglet to stand for his male chauvinist piggery. And then, finally, the match began.

The tennis itself was not without drama. King won her serve to open the match, and each player held serve until the fifth game, which Riggs won. But King broke Riggs's serve in the following game, demonstrating that she could bear down and beat him when she had to. At the end of the first set there was a point that King remembers as crucial. Riggs, whose specialty had always been putting his shots just where he wanted them rather than overpowering anybody, hit consecutive shots first deep to King's forehand corner, then deep to the backhand side. But King ran down both balls and got back into position to win the point. Moments later, she won the set, six games to four. In each of the next two sets, Riggs won only three games. The hustler had been outhustled in straight sets.

The immediate result was that Billie Jean King received a check for $100,000 — a particularly significant amount, since only a few years earlier she had become the first female player to make that much money in a year. The long-term effects of the King-Riggs match are difficult to measure, but its importance is undeniable. More people watched the contest than had ever before watched a tennis match. American bookmakers took bets on it, and it was the first time *they'd* ever paid any attention to tennis. Millions of people who wouldn't have recognized a top tennis pro on the street tuned in to King-Riggs that night. Some commentators credited King's victory with launching the boom tennis enjoyed over the next decade, and the winner agreed. "On that night," she said, "the game of tennis finally got kicked out of the country clubs forever and into the world of real sports."

It was ironic that a pseudo-match should have served that purpose, but no doubt Billie Jean King was right. The people watching her saw a feisty and energetic competitor, not the dainty ornament to the courts they might have expected. From the commentators they learned not only that King had been playing like that for years, but that she had been hammering in a most unladylike manner on the fools who'd dismissed women's tennis as a secondary attraction. The time was right for Billie Jean King, and after she beat Bobby Riggs, the American public embraced her enthusiastically. To King's delight, and to the delight of the other women on the tennis tour, the attention on King flooded over into the game that kept her employed.

Over the years that followed, Billie Jean King continued to test the limits of her game. She helped invent team tennis, which brought the sport new audiences. She battled the best players on the court, enduring knee operations and playing through other injuries for the opportunity. By the time she was ready to retire, she had won an unprecedented twenty Wimbledon titles. She had been nationally ranked in four different decades. She had taught millions of people how exciting tennis could be.

After she retired, Billie Jean King embarked on a new career as a tennis teacher. Her specialty was working with players who weren't living up to their potential, teaching them how to win. She worked with both men and women, helping them to develop confidence and competitive fire. "She is as daunting and revelatory as the headlights of an oncoming car," wrote *Sports Illustrated*'s Sally Jenkins of King at forty-seven, which would seem to suggest that she hadn't slowed down much. King's first prize pupil was the great Martina Navrati-lova, who was urged and bullied to break King's own Wimbledon-record twenty titles. A lesser player, a less energetic and committed champion, a lesser *person,* might want to hold on to a record like that. But holding on would imply standing still and looking backward, and Billie Jean King has never done much of either.

Diana Golden

Diana Golden is a world champion skier. She is a superb rock climber. She climbs mountains, too, and enjoys five-day solo treks through some of the most unforgiving desert in the country. Also, she has only one leg, though she probably won't mention it if you don't.

I was the last one picked on every team when I was a kid. I was a klutz. If you had ever told me that I would make being an athlete my profession, I would have laughed at you and my family would have laughed at you. They still laugh.

— Diana Golden

TWENTY-ODD YEARS beyond required gym class, Diana Golden still remembers what it felt like to be the last one picked for the basketball team, or the volleyball team, or any other team. "Come on," she used to say under her breath as the ranks of the unpicked grew thin, "pick me, come on."

According to her recollection, nobody ever did. That was part of what led her to embrace skiing as a child. You didn't have to be picked for it. You could do it by yourself. And it wasn't a required sport.

When she'd gotten pretty good at it, somebody suggested that Diana should try out for a kids' ski racing team. She made the team, but only lasted about two weeks. It was too serious. Too much competition. Too much like gym class. She returned to skiing for fun.

And then one day when she was twelve years old, Diana Golden's right leg collapsed under her. Weird, she thought. And then it happened again. When the doctors told her that the leg was cancerous and would have to be removed, she thought there had been some mistake. Cancer wasn't for twelve-year-olds. "Did you ask my grandfather?" she said. Granddaddy was a doctor, and he'd certainly tell these younger doctors they were wrong.

"He knows," they told her. "He agrees with us. We're sorry."

Diana Golden remembers that, after her surgery, she was brave while her parents and the doctors remained in the hospital room with her. But when they'd left her alone with her roommate, she cried for two hours. She couldn't remember ever seeing anyone with only one leg. She was sure her life would be a hopeless muddle of crutches, braces, mechanical legs, and pity from all quarters. But eventually she ran out of tears, and her roommate said, "Hey, when you have a fake leg, maybe you'll be able to turn your foot around backwards." And Diana laughed.

Over the days that followed, it occurred to Diana to ask one of her doctors if she'd still be able to ski. "No reason why not," the doctor said. That helped, too. How could she feel too sorry for herself if she could still ski? And how could she feel sorry for herself when so many of the other children in the hospital with her would never enjoy that opportunity, or any other?

"I saw teenagers die," she remembered years later. "I saw a two-year-old die. *That* was the stuff that was hard to understand. Given those things, I never felt bitter, never wondered 'Why me?' I was *living.*"

Within a few months after the removal of her leg, Diana Golden was back on the slopes. Of course she was still there on her own terms. She was a weekend hacker who liked skiing well enough to learn how to do it on one leg, but she was hardly inclined to train or work at it.

Through her first two years in high school, Diana Golden remained a weekend skier. She didn't train for competition, but given the circumstances, she couldn't help but develop some technique. As she has said since, "It didn't take me long to figure out there'd be no more snowplowing."

One afternoon during the winter of her junior year, a fellow in a ski parka and goggles flagged Diana Golden down on the slopes. When she'd skied up alongside him, she recognized the man as David Livermore, the skiing coach at Lincoln-Sudbury High School in Massachusetts, where Diana was a student. "Listen," Livermore said to her, "why don't you work out with the ski team?"

"He recruited me," Golden said later. "He's a perceptive man. He realized that the training would make a difference to me. He understood when he saw me skiing that I'd reached a point where working out, training, and pushing myself wouldn't be drudgery anymore. It wouldn't be gym class. And he was right. It was fun."

Within a few months Diana Golden, who had never done a push-up or a sit-up, was embarrassing the two-legged skiers with her workouts. "All of a sudden," as Golden remembered during a newspaper interview with Melanie Stephens years later, "I began to discover that I could train my body. It was wonderful. It was discovering the things that my body could do for me, discovering what it felt like to be strong."

By the winter of her senior year, Diana Golden had left klutziness so far behind that it was hard to remember the bad old days. The rigorous training to strengthen her leg, her back, and her arms felt not only right, but indispensable. And the progress the training produced was nothing short of astonishing. Only a year after taking David Livermore up on his suggestion, Diana Golden was competing in the World Games for Disabled Athletes in Geilo, Norway. Within the same year she won the downhill event in the World Handicapped Championships and became the brightest star on the United States Disabled Ski Team. She was skiing so well that, as *Boston Globe* sportswriter Tony Chamberlain put it, "She seemed *advantaged*." She had only one ski to worry about controlling, and she "moved back and forth down the hill with an unbroken motion as graceful as grass waving in a breeze."

That was, of course, an illusion. Skiing fast, like a lot of athletic feats, is harder than it looks. And skiing fast on one leg meant that Diana Golden had to cut from one edge of her ski to the other with more precision than most two-legged skiers could imagine. She had less margin for error because with one leg she had less opportunity to regain her balance when she lost it. Yet that sort of disadvantage never seemed to occur to Diana Golden. She was having too much fun to worry about it. She turned heads everywhere she skied, firing down the slopes like a wild bird, arms extended, snow flying everywhere. And the sense of fun was never eclipsed by the regimen of push-ups and sit-ups, or by the demands of competition. Once, at Vail, Colorado, when an out-of-control two-legged skier sent her sprawling and failed even to apologize, Golden bounced up, a look of mock horror spread across her face, and she shouted, "Hey, you! Look what you've done to my leg!"

By the time Diana Golden was ready to leave high school and enroll at Dartmouth College, the transformation was complete. "I was a total *anti*-klutz," she remembered. "Being a ski champion had become an image, the way I saw myself." She wasn't the only one who saw it that way. Even before she had graduated from high school, magazine and newspaper stories had begun to celebrate Diana Golden as not only a champion, but a hero, a role model, a courageous, inspirational athlete who had thumbed her nose at cancer and gone on not only to lead a full life but to win gold medals in the process.

Diana Golden didn't *feel* like a hero, though. She just felt like a skier who was doing her best to compete. Years later she would say, "What was heroic about me? People who stand up for what they believe are heroic. Martin Luther King. Nelson Mandela. Mother Theresa. Those are heroes . . . people who have done something wonderful for other people. I was just skiing fast." Sometimes the acclaim and the babbling about her courage got so strange that Golden could only laugh at it, like the time she was filling her car at a self-service station and the man behind the cash register, wide-eyed and well-meaning, told her how brave she was to be doing *that*.

The increasing gap between Diana Golden's view of herself and the public's perception of her as a courageous heroine created more pressure than any college sophomore should have to bear, and the difficulty was complicated by Golden's search for a spiritual center in her life. That search led her to embrace born-again Christianity, which in turn led to what Golden remembered as "a conflict between skiing and my desire to win on one hand, and my feeling of faith on the other. Skiing was one god, and God was another. I couldn't reconcile the demands of the two." Skiing began to make less and less sense. The praise heaped upon her in the sports columns and the magazine feature pieces rang more and more hollow. The attempt to figure out who she really was and what she wanted began to nudge training and racing out of Diana Golden's days.

Eventually Golden, who had practically defined herself through competitive skiing since David Livermore's fortuitous suggestion four years earlier, gave it up entirely. Over her last two years at Dartmouth, which is smack in the heart of New Hampshire's ski country, she skied only three times, and she never raced. She studied, read, and gradually began to understand herself as a person who *had* skied, rather than as a skier.

Then during her senior year it dawned on Diana Golden that to allow the media to define her or to warp her understanding of herself might stunt her own growth. She began to feel that it was crazy to have quit doing something she loved because the papers and television spots might misrepresent her efforts, or because of her inability to reconcile her faith with her athletic ambitions. As she said in retrospect, "I began to understand who I was under the roles I had taken." This isn't an easy thing for an athlete — particularly a very good athlete — to do. Young football players, basketball players, or skiers who constantly read about how brave, strong, and talented they are can have a hard time remembering that they are also fallible, entitled to goof, human.

For Diana Golden, that discovery didn't happen all at once, and when she graduated from Dartmouth, she wasn't ready to redevote herself absolutely to skiing. She took a job as a computer software salesperson. Personable, outgoing, and bright, she was good at her work. But before long she was bored. Maybe that's part of the reason she finally said "Sure" when some of her old friends proposed, for the umpteenth time, a ski weekend. Maybe they knew Diana well enough to figure that if they kept asking, she'd finally agree to go. But she surprised them once they'd all taken the lift to the top of the hill. In fact she delighted them by hopping with a giggle onto the slalom course on the slope and tearing through the gates with all the joy and enthusiasm that had characterized her championship runs. By the time she reached the bottom of the mountain, she was halfway hooked on skiing again. All she needed was a gentle push from one more friend, who told her, "When you're thirty, you can do anything you want, but you won't be winning races. Go for it now."

She did. Some of her expertise came back quickly, but the layoff meant she had to work harder than ever to strengthen her knee, leg, stomach, and arms again. She trained with other so-called "disabled" skiers, but also with the two-legged variety, whom Golden called the "normies." With each group she would pick out somebody who was a little faster, a little more confident, a little more successful than she was. Then she would work at narrowing the gap between their performances, and eventually she would leave most of her rivals in a shower of snow.

Soon Diana Golden realized that training was only part of the challenge. Because she wanted to compete all over the world against the best skiers she could find, she also had to work at finding a way to pay for the travel and living expenses. Sponsors! she thought, though this was an unprecedented notion for a disabled athlete. She went to the Rossignol Ski Company and said, "You guys back two-legged skiers all the time. You give them equipment. You finance their trips and pay their expenses so folks will see them winning races on your skis. Do the same for me. But don't do it because I ski on one leg. Do it because I'm going to win races. And every time I do it, there'll be a picture of your ski and your company logo on the sports page." Then she'd smile to close the deal.

If Rossignol had any doubts at the outset, they vanished in the glow of the results Diana Golden posted. As had been the case when David Livermore had first invited her to join the ski team, the timing was perfect. Diana Golden was ready to focus her concentration on becoming a great skier. Within a year of her return to competition in 1985, she won four gold medals. During the eighties she ran her totals to ten World Handicapped Championship golds and nineteen national championships. From 1986 to 1990 she monopolized the World Disabled skiing championships, and in 1988 she won an Olympic gold medal in the giant slalom for disabled skiers, which was a demonstration sport at the time.

Meanwhile, she was looking for other challenges. She started not only *training* alongside the skiers with two legs, but racing against them in formal competition, too. At first, entering the regular races was frustrating. "You can't imagine what it's like to come in first in a bunch of handicap races, then enter some two-legged race and come in last," Golden told the writers who were following her again. "But the really maddening thing was that I didn't get to ski until everybody else was finished and the course was a disaster, covered with deep ruts. It was then that I developed a fondness for Ben and Jerry's Heath Bar Crunch ice cream. It's good for depression."

Diana Golden's frustration and the undeniable excellence of her skiing led to a remarkable change in the rules that govern U.S. Ski Association competition. In 1985 the association decreed that, after the top fifteen skiers had performed in a given race, places would be reserved for disabled skiers competing in the event. The new arrangement was not only a great leap toward fairness, since it gave skiers like Diana Golden the chance to race over a course that was still intact; it also provided a model for other sports that would encourage people to view *all* the competitors as athletes, rather than seeing some of them as courageous wonders or superhuman curiosities. Naturally the change was instantly nicknamed the Golden Rule. And just as naturally, Diana Golden was the first athlete to take full advantage of it. Early in 1987, she finished tenth in a slalom race that included forty women, thirty-nine of whom were skiing on two legs. "That meant more to me than any medal I ever won, including the three golds at the World Championships in Sweden," Golden said, and it meant more to the sports community and the world at large as well. That tenth-place finish did a great deal to encourage the public to understand "disabled" athletes as *athletes* first.

Largely due to the efforts and the numerous triumphs of Diana Golden, that understanding has come to skiing more quickly and more thoroughly than it has come to most sports. In 1986, Golden won the Beck Award as the best American racer in international competition. In 1988, *Ski Racing* magazine named her U.S. Female Alpine Skier of the Year. Also in 1988, the U.S. Olympic Committee named her Female Skier of the Year. That was the year Golden was invited to be a forerunner for the prestigious and extraordinarily difficult Aspen World Cup Downhill Race. This meant she would test the course before the competition began, while the world's best skiers looked on. "There were no butterflies in my stomach that day," Golden remembered afterward.

There were snakes. And they lashed at me until I felt overwhelmed and half paralyzed. Just inspecting the course had given me the heebie-jeebies. It was far more difficult than any course I'd ever run. The greatest fear was that I might discover myself incapable, that I wouldn't be able to make it down and that the people who'd questioned my being there would be proved right. The pressure grew in intensity as I waited for my start number to be called. It kept building through the starter's command, "Racer ready," and through the countdown. But on the word "Go!" the pressure broke, as it had always in a big race. In that instant my mind and body took over and did precisely what they'd been trained to do for so many years. Through the course, gravity fought to pull me down, but I resisted it. My leg was giving out as I was coming through the bottom section. "Hold out! Hold out!" I yelled at myself. And then I was through the finish.

The titles Diana Golden won were not preceded by words like "disadvantaged" or "disabled." She had simply earned recognition as the best there was at what she did — which is what she'd been after all along. " 'Courageous' is my pet peeve," she told Meg Lukens for an article in *Sports Illustrated.* "I think it belittles our ability. I never wanted to be thought of as just having courage. I wanted to be recognized as a top-notch athlete, as the best in the world."

In 1991, at twenty-seven, Diana Golden retired from competitive skiing. She'd won more gold medals than she could carry, and now other challenges beckoned. She took up rock climbing and announced her intention to coach skiers — "both the one-legged and the two-legged kind." She said she wanted to bring credibility to "disabled ski instructors — not just as teachers of other disabled people, but of anyone." She treked off alone into the Utah desert for five days, testing herself against heat, cold, exhaustion, and loneliness, charging along on two forearm crutches until she found the reward she'd intuitively known the trip would provide. "It was just beautiful," she said of that adventure. "I was out there alone, with the sun on my back, and it was as if I could smell everything around me — the cliffs, the ruins. It seemed like I was taking everything in one sensual rush. I wasn't small, frail, and vulnerable. I was tough, strong, and indomitable. I was capable."

When she returned home she had once again made an opportunity of what most people would consider an obstacle, but Diana Golden wouldn't call the trek a big deal. She'd leave that for others. And when they said she was "courageous" and even "heroic," she'd patiently sit down with them and explain why that wasn't it at all.

Roberto Clemente

Once, years ago, during a cold rain that was about to force the postponement of a baseball game, Jim Woods, an old radio announcer who'd worked for the Giants, the Yankees, the Athletics, and half the rest of the teams in the game was remembering the greatest players he'd known. "I saw Willie Mays and Duke Snider in their primes," he said, "and over here in the American League I saw Mickey Mantle and Carl Yastrzemski, too. And I wouldn't want to make any of 'em mad by saying which one was the best. But the guy I'd pay to see in the outfield every day was Roberto Clemente."

I would forget to eat because of baseball.
— Roberto Clemente
on his childhood

AS A SMALL BOY in Carolina, Puerto Rico, Roberto Clemente was not the guy you went looking for if you wanted an errand done. Even his mother couldn't count on him. "I'd send him to the store and he'd be gone for hours," she remembered years later. "He'd have found a baseball game somewhere."

Baseball had come to the island with the U.S. Marines, as it had come to much of the rest of Latin America beginning in the second half of the nineteenth century. And as in the Dominican Republic, Cuba, and Mexico, in Puerto Rico the game represented one of the few things that nearly everyone could agree was good about that big, hungry uncle of a nation to the north, *los Estados Unidos,* the United States. As Kal Wagenheim, one of Clemente's biographers put it, "Imperialism was sinful. Politics was controversial — some Puerto Ricans embraced the U.S. flag, others despised it, and most were confused. But *beisbol* [baseball] was fun."

Certainly young Roberto Clemente wouldn't have argued with the part about baseball. When he couldn't find a game, he practiced by throwing a rubber ball against the wall of his house, trying to simulate grounders, line drives, and pop-ups. And when he *could* find a game, he never let the lack of official equipment slow him down. When he was eight years old he was playing with a bat carved from a guava tree. His glove was only an old coffee sack, but the ball didn't sting his hand any. It was just a wad of rags he'd tied together as tightly as he could. Fortunately the scouts who spent their time nosing around the island neighborhoods for promising ballplayers were no more hung up on details like what the ball was made of than Roberto and his friends were. When the future Hall of Famer was fourteen, a scout named Roberto Marin recruited Clemente for a top amateur team because he'd been impressed by how far the kid could hit empty tomato cans with a stick.

Tin cans, rubber balls, or the real thing, Roberto Clemente could hit them all. And he could catch anything anybody else hit, too, even if he had to run forever to do it. And then he could throw. Maybe that's what he could do best of all. Certainly that's the baseball skill of which he was most proud. When Clemente played with the Santurce Crabbers in the Puerto Rican Winter League in the early fifties, it was his arm that most impressed the fellow playing beside him in center field. That fellow was Willie Mays, who had already achieved stardom as a member of the New York Giants. Many would claim Mays was the best outfielder the game had ever seen, and Willie certainly knew talent when he saw it. He knew the teenaged Clemente in right was already throwing harder and more accurately than most of the outfielders in the big leagues.

Unfortunately for the Giants, Willie didn't have the authority to sign young Clemente to a contract. But the Dodger scout on hand, Al Campanis, did. In February 1954, at the age of nineteen, Clemente signed with the Dodgers for a ten-thousand-dollar bonus and a salary of five thousand a year. "Find yourself a nice woman to marry, and settle down with her," the owner of the Dodgers told his newest employee, "then you can concentrate on being the superstar you're going to be." Roberto's father had some less grandiose advice to offer: "Buy yourself a good car and don't depend on anybody," don Melchor Clemente said. "*Adios y buenos suerte.*" (Good-bye and good luck.)

The Dodgers sent Roberto to their top minor league club in Montreal, where he quickly discovered the difference between playing at home and playing on the road. "I had studied English in high school, but I never really had to speak it until I joined the team in Montreal," Clemente remembered during an interview for the Wagenheim biography. His initial efforts at a new language were uneven. One day he made an especially spectacular catch in right field, turning an apparent extra-base hit into a harmless out and ending the inning. As he trotted in from the outfield, he passed the player who'd hit the ball.

"You son of a bitch," the hitter muttered.

"Thank you," Roberto replied.

Though his understanding of the language and his ability to speak English would improve over the years, the writers and even his managers would sometimes ridicule him for his imperfect speech. Danny Murtaugh, who managed the Pirates, once told a group of writers that Clemente had returned to the bench after an at-bat in which he'd bunted and said, "Boss, me no feel like home run." Murtaugh knew it would get a laugh. Throughout his career, Clemente bitterly resented the tendency he found everywhere for Americans to belittle, mock, and underrate Latins like himself. He fought it constantly, and sometimes poignantly. When he was interviewed after his team had won the 1971 World Series, he interrupted the broadcaster who was asking him a question in English and asked his parents' blessing in his native Spanish. Then he said, "I love the poor people, the workers, the minority people, the ones who suffer. They have a different outlook on life."

Of course, before he could say to several million people something so unlike what all the other players in the locker room were saying, Roberto Clemente had to make it out of Montreal, which was a cut above the Puerto Rican Winter League, but still a minor league town. He did it in an unusual way. Dodger fans are still shaking their heads about it nearly half a century after the fact. Because although scout Al Campanis had convinced the Dodgers to sign the brilliant outfielder, they did not promote him from Montreal to Brooklyn that season. Under the "bonus rule" — which said that any player who'd received more than four thousand dollars to sign and who wasn't playing in the major leagues could be drafted by another organization — Roberto Clemente was up for grabs in the fall. The Pittsburgh Pirates had finished last that season and had first shot at the cream of the minor league crop. Without hesitation they drafted Clemente, who would play his entire career in Pittsburgh. The saddest side of that remarkable transaction is the implication that the Dodgers management didn't protect their prize youngster because they already had all the black players they could handle at the time. Even the club that had broken the color line by hiring Jackie Robinson in 1947 may not have been ready to field a team on which the black players outnumbered the whites.

The Pittsburgh team Roberto Clemente joined in 1955 was hopeless. During the fifties the Pirates finished last five times, and next to last three times. But from the first time Clemente came to the plate, when he slammed a single off Dodgers pitcher Johnny Podres, the Pirate fans knew they'd at least have one player to celebrate. He ran and hit and threw with apparently effortless grace, but the people who followed the team closely knew there was nothing effortless about Clemente's success. They knew that he practiced by the hour taking batted balls off the quirky right-field fence in Forbes Field, just as he'd practiced catching the rubber ball that had bounced off the side of his house back in Carolina, Puerto Rico.

They knew, too, that before Clemente had ever set foot in a big league ballpark, an automobile accident in which a drunken driver had skidded into his car had injured his back. In order to play at all, he had to exercise and stretch continually, as well as endure countless treatments. Each time he came to the plate, he'd twist and turn and stretch his neck like a man whose collar was too tight. He spent so much time with chiropractors and physical therapists that eventually he became something of an expert on bad backs, and during the winter in Puerto Rico, people in pain would stagger to his door at all hours for help. Clemente never turned them away. He'd tell them to lie down on the pool table in his basement, then he would knead their sore muscles and work their crooked spines straight. Many swore that he had magic in his hands.

Playing for the Pirates not only meant that Roberto Clemente was stuck with a bad team, at least for a time. It also meant that he would labor in a small market. While the big publicity machines were grinding out celebrations of players in New York, Los Angeles, Boston, and other prominent cities, Clemente and his teammates played in relative obscurity. When it came time to count the votes for the league's most valuable player award each year, this quick and powerful outfielder who led the National League in hitting no fewer than four times would often come up short. Clemente read the failure of the writers to recognize his talent and hard work as a snub, and chastised them for ignoring Latin players who could not easily express themselves in English. Sometimes well-meaning interviewers would try to compliment the Pirate star by comparing him to Willie Mays, who played in New York (and later San Francisco) and never lacked for publicity. "You play like Willie," they'd say with a smile.

"No," Clemente would tell them solemnly, "I play only like Roberto Clemente."

Over the years Roberto Clemente's pride drove a fierce insistence that writers, broadcasters, and others on the fringes of baseball's world take him seriously as a man, a Puerto Rican, and a ballplayer. As surely as Jackie Robinson had been a model for black American players, Clemente led the way for Latins from his homeland, as well as from the Dominican Republic, Venezuela, and other Latin countries beginning to supply talent to the big leagues. And to those fortunate enough to see him play each day, Roberto Clemente offered another side. Even when he was in pain, he could make fun of himself. Only a few years into his career, he was already notorious for the routine of stretching and craning his neck that preceded each Clemente at-bat.

The chronic spinal problem made it impossible for him to avoid these contortions, which some observers felt were melodramatic. The same people gave Clemente a hard time for complaining about the injuries he regularly catalogued, but sometimes he would zing them back. During a game in July 1960, Clemente, who had been complaining of a sore foot, scored all the way from first base on a pop-up single. After the game, before any of the writers could bring up the discrepancy between his pregame litany of aches and pains and his dash around the bases, Clemente told them, "My foot was sore. I ran all the way home so I could rest it on the bench."

The Pirates climbed on Roberto Clemente's coattails shortly after he arrived in Pittsburgh, and in the matter of a few short years, he showed them how to be winners. Still, the baseball world was shocked when Pittsburgh won the World Series in 1960, even if Clemente wasn't. He led the team in hitting and played right field flawlessly. But he was unsatisfied with his own performance, and during the winter he promised his parents that he would become the best hitter in all of baseball.

In 1961 he did just that, leading the league with an average of .351. He would hit .300 or better for ten of the next eleven years, over which he would also accumulate three thousand hits, a milestone reached by only the greatest and most durable hitters in the game's history, such as Ty Cobb, Pete Rose, and, incidentally, Willie Mays. He would also collect an impressive list of compliments from the men who played against him. Sandy Koufax, the superb Dodger lefthander, admitted that he hated to pitch to Clemente above all other hitters, because Clemente had no weaknesses. "He could hit a pitchout for a home run," Koufax once complained.

Still, because Pittsburgh was a small media market and because the Pirates did not return to the World Series during the sixties, relatively few fans gave Clemente the credit he deserved, though in Puerto Rico he was lionized. But sometimes events conspire to arrange a perfect meeting of man and opportunity, and when the Pirates made it to the fall classic again in 1971, that's what happened to Roberto Clemente. By then he was thirty-seven years old, and he had talked of retirement many times, though he'd hit .341 during the season. In the National League playoffs, where Pittsburgh beat the Giants, Clemente hit .333. He was only warming up. Against the Orioles in the World Series, he hit .414, slammed two home runs, knocked in four runs, and made enough game-saving plays in right field to make them seem routine. In game two, which the Orioles won 11–3, Clemente threw a perfect strike to third base to try to nail Merv Rettenmond, who was advancing on a sacrifice fly. It was a great play in the middle of a lost cause. Another player on a team that far behind might have lobbed the ball in and saved his arm, but Roberto Clemente always played baseball as it was meant to be played. At the end of the day the Orioles led the series two games to none, but the image of Roberto Clemente's perfect throw hung in the air of the empty ballpark as if to suggest that, contrary to the evidence of the score, Clemente's Pirates weren't finished yet.

On the plane back to Pittsburgh, Clemente urged his teammates to pay no attention to the sports pages, where the writers were all predicting Baltimore's victory. "Do not read the newspapers and you will see. We will win," he assured them. Then he proceeded to show them exactly how it could be done, and he was at his creative best. Over the remainder of the series, he hit a triple, two doubles, and two home runs. Maybe lots of players could have done that. But late in game three, with Pittsburgh clinging to a one-run lead, when he tapped a routine ground ball back to the mound, Roberto Clemente did more. It should have been an easy out, but Clemente ran so hard down the first-base line that he surprised Oriole pitcher Mike Cuellar into a bad throw. The Pirates built Clemente's act of determination into a rally that finished off Baltimore in that game and put the series up for grabs. After game seven, when the dust around home plate had settled for the winter, it was the Pirates who'd grabbed the victory, and Clemente who had led them. Roger Angell, that most eloquent of writers on baseball, said of Clemente then: "He played a kind of baseball that none of us had ever seen before — throwing and running and hitting at something close to the level of absolute perfection, playing to win but also playing the game almost as if it were a form of punishment for everyone else on the field." During the series Clemente had told Angell, "I want everybody in the world to know that this is the way I play all the time. All season, every season. I give everything I have to this game."

The following year, 1972, Roberto Clemente's average fell to .312, and though that would have been excellent for most players, he was disappointed. His Pirates had lost to the Cincinnati Reds in the National League Championship Series. He told friends he was planning to return for one more season. But meanwhile he was devoting himself to an exhausting array of off-season causes. There were speaking engagements and other commitments in the States that kept him constantly in transit, and though he did not like having to leave his wife, his children, and his parents in Puerto Rico, he realized that his growing fame carried with it many responsibilities. When he *was* home, his informal back clinic continued to thrive at all hours. Word of the tender strength of his hands had spread. And beyond all this he had developed the idea that the Puerto Rican government should establish a Sports City in San Juan, a place where poor children could learn baseball and other games without charge. He imagined a place of many fields and many coaches and many eager young ballplayers, and he'd begun lobbying for the Sports City with the same drive and enthusiasm that had fueled his own baseball career.

Then, on December 23, there was news of a catastrophe that would erase from Roberto Clemente's schedule every other concern. An earthquake in Nicaragua killed six thousand people, injured twenty thousand more, and left three thousand without homes. Clemente had visited Nicaragua, most recently only a month before, when he had managed Puerto Rico's team in the World Series of Amateur Baseball. He had made many friends there. Beyond that, the Nicaraguans, like Latins elsewhere, were his *compañeros*, his brothers.

As soon as he heard about the earthquake, Clemente began working with other Puerto Ricans who were collecting food, clothing, and medical supplies for transport to Managua, the Nicaraguan capital. Well aware of the power of his name, he made personal pleas over radio and television, and in response men and women all over Puerto Rico donated all they could.

Soon huge shipments of aid were on the way by sea and by air. But after the first planes had landed, disturbing reports began coming back to San Juan. There were rumors of irregularities in the distribution of the relief supplies. Some said the authorities charged with getting the goods to the injured and homeless earthquake victims were inefficient, and there were even reports that the authorities were stealing supplies for themselves. Feeling that perhaps his presence would deter that sort of misconduct, Clemente determined to accompany the next shipment. On the night of December 31, he climbed into a patched-up DC-7 cargo plane. It was overloaded with baby formula and hospital supplies. It was twenty years old and in dubious repair. Its departure was delayed several times while a mechanic fussed with its cranky engines. In fact, at one point the impatient Clemente told a friend at the airport, "One more delay and I won't go tonight. I'll wait until tomorrow." But then the engines sputtered into life, the pilot waved for Clemente to board again, and the plane began wobbling down the runway. A few minutes after takeoff, one engine began vibrating and another caught fire. The pilot banked the DC-7 to the left, perhaps trying to circle the airport and land, but he never made it. A little before 9:30 P.M., the plane fell off the airport radar screen and into the sea. The pilot's body was recovered a few days later, but Roberto Clemente's body was never found.

Clemente's death left his wife and children devastated and plunged all Puerto Rico into grief. The inauguration of the governor was postponed, and when Rafael Hernández Colón finally did take office, a day late, he began his speech by saying, "Our people have lost one of their glories."

Meanwhile the Pittsburgh Pirates and all of baseball also mourned. They had lost a teammate, a giant within the game. But they had also lost a proud and brave friend, a man worthy of their respect and love as well as their admiration. In Hispanic neighborhoods across the country, shocked fans marched in silent tribute. Roberto Clemente's untimely death had moved them as the death of few athletes have ever moved a people.

New Year's Day 1973 was gray and rainy that year in Puerto Rico. It was as if, as one newspaper columnist wrote, "even the sky was in mourning." Sportswriters in the United States were stirred as well. They voted to suspend the rule that prevented a player from entering the Hall of Fame until he'd been out of the game for five years. Roberto Clemente was enshrined in Cooperstown on March 20, 1973. He was the first Latin player to be so honored. The long and illustrious parade of his *compañeros* to follow could not have had a more splendid leader.

Suggested Reading

SATCHEL PAIGE

Maybe I'll Pitch Forever, Leroy (Satchel) Paige, as told to David Lipman, Doubleday and Company, New York, 1962.

Invisible Men: Life in Baseball's Negro Leagues, Donn Rogosin, Atheneum, New York, 1983.

Blackball Stars: Negro League Pioneers, John B. Holway, Meckler Corp., Westport, Conn., 1988.

JULIE KRONE

Riding for My Life, Julie Krone with Nancy Ann Richardson, Little, Brown and Company, Boston, 1995.

"She who laughs last . . ." Gary Smith, *Sports Illustrated,* May 22, 1989.

PELÉ

Pelé, World Soccer Star, Julian May, Crestwood House, Inc., Mankato, Minn., 1975.

Pelé: A Biography, James S. Haskins, Doubleday and Company, New York, 1976.

"Pelé: The Black Pearl Remains More Than an Athlete," Joel Millman, *Sport,* December 1986.

JOAN BENOIT SAMUELSON

Running Tide, Joan Benoit (with Sally Baker), Knopf, New York, 1987.

NATE "TINY" ARCHIBALD

Tiny: The Story of Nate Archibald, John Devaney, G. P. Putnam's Sons, New York, 1977.

"Down to the Bitter . . . but Oh-So-Sweet End," *Boston Globe,* May 18, 1981.

"Tiny Still Specializes in Making Assists," Franz Lidz, *Sports Illustrated,* February 11, 1991.

SUSAN BUTCHER

"A Woman and Her Dogs," Susan Trausch, *Boston Globe Magazine,* October 18, 1987.

Body and Soul: Ten American Women, Text by Carolyn Coman, Photographs by Judy Dater, Hill and Company, Boston, 1988.

"Man's Best Friends," Robert F. Jones, *Sports Illustrated,* March 27, 1989.

Woodsong, Gary Paulsen, Bradbury Press, New York, 1990.

"The Dogged Pursuit of Excellence," Sonja Steptoe, *Sports Illustrated,* February 11, 1991.

MUHAMMAD ALI

Muhammad Ali: His Life and Times, Thomas Hauser, Simon and Schuster, New York, 1991.

BILLIE JEAN KING

Billie Jean, Billie Jean King, with Kim Chapin, Harper and Row, New York, 1974.

Billie Jean, Billie Jean King, with Frank Deford, Viking Press, New York, 1982.

My Life with the Pros, Bud Collins, Dutton, New York, 1989.

"Racket Science," Sally Jenkins, *Sports Illustrated,* April 29, 1991.

DIANA GOLDEN

"Golden Girl — That's Diana Golden, U.S. Three-Track Ski Racer Extraordinaire," Peter Miller, *Skiing,* November 1987.

"Golden Time: Disabled Skier Is Savoring Spotlight," *Boston Globe,* February 21, 1988.

"Golden Demonstrates Her Ability," Kevin Paul Dupont, *Boston Globe,* February 22, 1988.

"Skiing a Formidable Course," Meg Lukens, *Sports Illustrated,* December 31, 1990.

"A Golden Triumph in Uphill Battle," Tony Chamberlain, *Boston Globe,* February 10, 1991.

"Golden Voice," Kevin Paul Dupont, *Boston Globe,* August 20, 1991.

ROBERTO CLEMENTE

"Some Pirates and Lesser Men," in *The Summer Game,* Roger Angell, Viking Press, New York, 1972.

Clemente: The Life of Roberto Clemente, Kal Wagenheim, Pocket Books, New York, 1974.

The World Series: A Complete Pictorial History, John Devaney and Burt Goldblatt, Rand McNally, Chicago, 1981.

El Beisbol: Travels Through the Pan-American Pastime, John Krich, Atlantic Monthly Press, New York, 1989.

Index

Ali, Muhammad, x, 33, 81–92
Anderson-Schiess, Gabriela, 49
Archibald, Nate ("Tiny"), x, 53–66
athletes
  after career has ended, 52, 64, 91–92, 103–
    104, 116
  community service of
    Archibald's, xi, 53, 54, 62, 64, 66
    Clemente's, 121, 122–123, 127–128
    Pelé's, 37–38
  disabled, x, xi, 105–116
  and education, x, 58–60, 64
  and endorsements, 37–38, 112, 114
  as heroes, vii–ix
  injuries of, 23–24, 30–31, 44–52, 74, 91–
    92, 103, 122–125
  motivations of, 14–15, 40, 41, 55, 71, 109
  pitfalls for, viii, 12, 110–111
  qualities important in, 23–24, 34, 39, 40,
    41, 45, 55, 60, 74, 87
  on winning, x, 45, 51

baseball, xi, 1–10, 98, 117–129
basketball, 53–66
Benoit, Joan, x, 39–52
Bird, Larry, 60, 63
Bonventre, Pete, 91
boxing, 81–92
Butcher, Susan, x, 67–80

Campanis, Al, 120, 121
Chamberlain, Tony, 109
Clemente, Roberto, ix, 117–129
Collins, Bud, 96, 98, 100, 101
Court, Margaret Smith, 98, 100, 102
Cousy, Bob, 60–61

disabled athletes, x, xi, 105–116
dog sled racing, 67–80
Dundee, Angelo, 84, 90–91

Foreman, George, 89–91

Golden, Diana, x, xi, 105–116

Haskins, James, 33
horse racing, x, 11–24

Jenkins, Sally, 103
jockeys, 11–24

King, Billie Jean, x, xi, 93–104
Koufax, Sandy, 125
Krone, Julie, x, 11–24
Kubitschek de Oliveira, Juscelino, 30

Lane, Floyd, 58–60, 62
Liston, Sonny, 83–86, 91
Livermore, David, 108–109, 111, 114

McBurney, Linda, 24
Mailer, Norman, 91
Marin, Roberto, 120
Marquez, Armando, 22
Mays, Willie, 117, 120, 123, 125
Migliore, Richie, 23
Murtaugh, Danny, 121

Nascimento, Edson Arantes do. *See* Pelé
Navratilova, Martina, 104
Negro leagues, 1, 4, 6–8, 10

Olympics, 39, 41, 44–47, 49–50, 83, 85

Pace, Jerry, 16
Paige, Leroy "Satchel," x, xi, 1–10
Paulsen, Gary, 76
Pelé, x, 25–38
poverty, x, 27–28, 55, 58, 119–120
prejudice. *See* racism; sexism

racism
  against blacks, x, xi, 7–8, 9, 10, 85–86,
    122
  against Latins, 120–121, 123
Redington, Joe, 71–72, 74–75
Riggs, Bobby, 94, 99–103
Robinson, Jackie, x, 4, 8, 122
Rodgers, Bill, 49–50
Rujano, Miguel, 19
runners, 39–52
Ruth, Babe, 7, 25, 35

Samuelson, Joan Benoit, x, 39–52
sexism, x, xi, 14–15, 19, 22, 46–47, 77
skiers, 105–116
soccer, 25–38
Swenson, Rick, 77

tennis, xi, 93–104

Wagenheim, Kal, 119, 121
Waitz, Grete, 47, 49
Woods, Jim, 117